COMMUNITY OUTREACH FOR YOUTH SUCCESS

NURTURING THE HEALTH OF YOUTH

WILLIE JAMES WEBB

COMMUNITY OUTREACH FOR YOUTH SUCCESS

NURTURING THE HEALTH OF YOUTH

WILLIE JAMES WEBB

ISBN: 979-8-9907506-8-5
ISBN: 979-8-9907506-9-2

Independently Published by Willie James Webb

TABLE OF CONTENTS

INTRODUCTION

This book is based on the research, studies and professional practice of Willie James Webb in his roles as probation officer, probation/parole supervisor, project-director and correction specialist in county, state and federally funded juvenile and criminal justice programs. This book is also based on the passionate concern that Webb has for the safe and healthy development and growth of children and a secure society for all people. Webb's work in juvenile justice allied him closely with the public-school systems in Atlanta and Fulton County, Georgia. Most of the research on recidivism was done with students of the Atlanta and Fulton County School systems. Although his research was done between 1964 and 1975, the basic theses and principles remain valid, and probably, more relevant and more needed today than ever before. This book will be very helpful and insightful for any person, agency or institution that wish to get an in depth understanding of the core problems and root causes of delinquency and crime. It also will provide great insight on how to establish and administer community outreach social and human services programs.

This volume will bring an awareness to the vast societal changes that have taken place between 1964 and 2013. In the 1960's the word, "Negro," was in common use for race designation for the black American population. However, the Civil Rights movement spawn the use of the racial terminologies of Black American and African-American beginning in the late 1960's to the present time. Another societal change in Atlanta, was the discontinuation and demolition of Atlanta Housing Projects where high concentrations of low socioeconomic citizens lived. They were predominately Black. Most of the Juvenile Court's Community Outreach Programs were located in the Housing Projects. Another great change was and is the use of the computer, social media, the internet, Facebook, Twitter and the many uses of cell phones. However, when it comes to delinquency and crime, the common folk saying is still applicable, "The more things change, the more they remain the same."

It is important for the reader of this book to be aware that this information in Part One and Part Two were developed over a ten year period, from 1964 to 1975. This was during the decade when the Southern United States, including Atlanta Fulton County, Georgia were transitioning from a racially segregated society to desegregation. These racial social dynamics were very much involved during the compilation of the contents of this book. Part One of this book is based on Webb's Thesis at Atlanta University, in 1970. Part Two is based on his Thesis at Georgia State University, in 1976. The most helpful professor advising Webb at AU was Dr. Tilman Cothran. The most helpful professor at GSU in the Thesis advisement was a professor by the name of Dr. Francis Bridges. He was a fair-minded White male. Race is pointed out here to highlight the many white individuals who were very helpful during this racial transition period.

The significant contribution of this book will indicate and reinforce the social characteristics involved in juvenile offenses and crimes. Since these factors can be isolated and studied, they can be used as predictive factors to control, prevent and minimize delinquent behaviors and criminal offenses. Another significant contribution of this work is to show the vital importance of creating an ethical, professional and healthy administrative atmosphere in these juvenile justice, criminal justice, mental health and other social and human service agencies. Such an administrative atmosphere creates high morale among staff. It allows them to place major emphasis and time on the clients instead of the self-protective defensive mode of having the need to take care of themselves from a dysfunctional administrative agency. A healthy personnel administration generates and unleashes the energy and interest of the staff to be creative and innovative in carrying out their duties and responsibilities for the clients and the objectives and goals of the agency. Part Three of this book will provide some insight into the social and cultural contexts of present-day problems and some treatment approaches, skills and resources that can be utilized to bring about the desperately needed youth transformation.

The author wishes to acknowledge the vast number of people who were involved in the research, studies and intimate and personal work involvement of this project. It is not possible to acknowledge everyone by name. The thousands of youth and their families, the associated agencies and individuals from school systems and other agencies are acknowledged. The fine staff of probation officers and other support staff at the Juvenile Court are acknowledged. The author of this book was highly motivated and inspired by the supervisors, administrators and clerical staff of the (Impact) Community Outreach Program. It was an awesome community outreach team.

Judge John S. Langford, Jr. played a major role as the Chief Judge at the Fulton County Juvenile Court. He hired the first two Black Court Referees, Romae Powell and George Geiger. They both became the first two Black Judges of the Juvenile Court. He promoted the first Black Chief Probation

Officer. He promoted Willie J. Webb as one of the first Black Supervisors to supervise an integrated professional staff. He also promoted Webb as the first Investigative Supervisor and the first Community Outreach Supervisor that paved the way for a multi-million dollar grant for the LEAA (Law Enforcement Assistance Administration) Impact Program. Judge Langford sent his children to Morris Brandon Elementary School in the Buckhead area of Atlanta. Hundreds of the Atlanta Housing Projects children were bussed to Morris Brandon. A great White Principal by the name of Zerah Baggett accepted those children and integrated them in such a professional way that Morris Brandon's number-one rating did not go down. This same Principal accepted Wilma Webb as the first Black teacher at Brandon and also Karen Webb (daughter of the Author and Wilma) without any problems. Judge Langford and Principal Baggett were two outstanding white leaders during the integration transition in the 1960's and 1970's. There were other helpful personnel in the persons of Chief Probation Officers, Dr. Robert Croom, Mr. J. D Fleming, Coordinator, Wilma Turner and the Criminal Analysis Team from LEAA. ARC, Judy Dunn. State and the City of Atlanta.

New Possibilities for Juvenile Justice contains invaluable information for all persons and agencies that desire to gain helpful knowledge of juvenile problems and what can be done to fix them and prevent them. The Juvenile Court's Community Outreach Program engaged a host of schools, churches and other community agencies.

One of the Outreach offices was located in the Wheat Street Gardens Housing Complex of the historic Wheat Street Baptist Church of Atlanta under the pastorate of The Reverend William Holmes Borders, Sr. The knowledge of this book is based on a cross section of agencies and professionals with years of working experience with the juvenile population represented, including the social and faith-based institutions. The Author is encouraging with urgency for the social, educational, faith based and other youth-oriented organizations to get seriously and massively and redemptively involved in rescuing and saving the most vulnerable and at-risk youth of America.

The Author who is the Pastor of Foundation Baptist Church of Atlanta and who chairs the Committee for Clergy Training of Concerned Black Clergy of Atlanta is soliciting massive involvement in the remediation, prevention, support and growth of the youth of Atlanta and the Nation. This book is a source and a foundation for taking bold initiatives to save all of God's children. The author wishes to express thanks to P. J. Davenport for her efficiency and conscientious efforts in typing and putting this manuscript together.

LIST OF TABLES

PART ONE
AN ANALYSIS OF THE
SOCIAL CHARACTERISTICS OF RECIDIVIST

PART ONE

AN ANALYSIS OF THE SOCIAL CHARACTERISTICS OF RECIDIVISTS

CHAPTER I
INTRODUCTION

The problem of recidivism among juveniles is at the very core of the whole problem of juvenile delinquency. The juveniles who continue to recidivate after treatment and other corrective measures form the bulk of the high hardcore caseloads of most probation and parole officers. It is apparent also that the recidivists increase significantly in the intake of delinquent cases by their persistence in delinquency, frequently involving companions in their delinquent activities. Maude M. Craig and Laila A. Bud' conducted a study on recidivism and companions, and found that offenses committed with the aid of companions ranged from twenty-five percent (25%) to ninety-one percent (91%) of all cases depending on the age and seriousness of the offense. The study indicated that companionship in delinquent acts increases proportionately with age and the seriousness of the offense.

Recidivism tends to aggravate and play havoc with the primary purpose of probation and parole systems—basically to prevent recidivism. Generally, a treatment technique (probation, commitment to an institution or parole) is considered completely successful if no treated offenders recidivate. However, recidivism, according to authoritative sources, ranges from forty percent (40%) to seventy percent (70%) among such offenders.

Recidivism is one of the crucial phenomena in criminal and delinquent behavior. Unlike the first offender, whose identity was unknown before his first offense, and whose offense was unpredictable from a probability standpoint, the recidivist is well known and therefore, should be under administrative control, since by definition, "a recidivist is a person who, having been convicted and subject to correctional treatment, again commits a crime?

It might be noted at this point that recidivism varies with method and definition. Recidivism is defined generally in such terms as, "the persistent offender," "the repeaters" and "the habitual criminal." Other methods used in applying the label recidivism, refer to the number of times the person was arrested or taken into custody by the police or the number of times the person was referred to the juvenile court or correctional authorities. Some authorities insist that only a juvenile who commits repeated delinquent acts should be termed a juvenile delinquent. Various definitions of recidivism are used in the various studies.

The terms, "recidivist" and "repeater" are used synonymously in most instances. However, additional investigation into the meaning of the two terms, revealed that they carry a slightly different connotation. According to Norval Morris" "recidivist," carries the idea of temporary cure. He defines recidivism as, "The habit of relapsing into crime," and "relapse" as "a falling back into error, heresy or wrongdoing—the fact of falling back again into illness after a partial recovery." H. M. Metcalf defines "recidivism," as a falling back or relapse into prior criminal habits, especially after punishment."

For the purpose of this study, the concept of "recidivist" will be considered over against the concept of "repeater." The writer acknowledges that the two concepts overlap at points, and concedes that it is not necessary to strictly construe the two concepts for the purpose of this study based on the samples for analysis.

The following definitions to be considered in this study are excerpted from the Georgia Juvenile Court Act of 1951.5.

According to the Juvenile Court Act of 1951 as amended through 1968 by the 1968 session of the General Assembly of Georgia:

"Child" means a person less than seventeen (17) years of age.

"Adult" means a person seventeen (17) years of age or older.

"Delinquent Child" shall mean any person under the age of seventeen (17) years who:

1. Commits an act, which if committed by an adult, would be a crime, under federal or state law, or a violation of a municipal ordinance or law;
2. Is corrigible, ungovernable or habitually disobedient and beyond the control of his parent, guardian other custodian;
3. Is in violation of the compulsory school attendance law;
4. Without just cause without the consent of his parent, guardian, or other custodian, deserts his home or place of abode;
5. Engages in an occupation or whose behavior, condition, environment, or associations are such as to endanger his health, morals, or general welfare or that of others;
6. Associates with immoral or vicious persons;
7. Frequents a place the existence of which is in violation of the law;
8. Is found begging, receiving or gathering alms, whether actually begging or under the pretest of selling or offering anything for sale: Provided, this shall not be construed to prohibit solicitation on behalf of a recognized agency;

9. Unaccompanied by parent, patronizes or visits any bar where intoxicating liquors are sold; or is found in possession of intoxicating liquor;
10. Wanders or loiters about the streets of any city, or in or about any highway or any public place between the hours of twelve (12:00) o'clock midnight and five (5:00) o'clock A.M.;
- (f) The singular includes the plural, the plural the singular, and masculine the feminine, when consistent with the intent of the Act.

"Probationer," is a person who has been adjudicated delinquent and placed under the supervision of the court by order of the Judge.

"Child" and "juvenile" in this study are used interchangeably with "parolee" and probationer.

The problem - There has been no descriptive study of recidivism at the Fulton County Juvenile Court up to this present time. This study is designed to obtain factual information concerning a randomly selected number of recidivists at Fulton County Juvenile Court and give an analysis of a number of social characteristics relating to the recidivist population.

This study consists of a sample of forty (40) boys who were placed on probation and parole in 1969 by original court order, and who have subsequently committed additional acts of delinquency since being placed under the supervision of the court. The sample, which was obtained by a stratified random selection, includes seventeen (17) Negro probationers, eleven 11) Negro parolees, ten (10) white probationers and two (2) white parolees. The sample was obtained from a population of five hundred fifty-five (555) probationers and one hundred forty-five (145) parolees who were placed under the supervision of the court by original court order in 1969. All of the recidivists were on active supervision at the conclusion of this research in June 1970. All of the recidivists have received some type of corrective treatment after having been placed on probation and parole.

Purpose of the study - The purpose of this study is to (1) isolate a selected number of social characteristics of juvenile recidivists; (2) to investigate the characteristics for any tendency toward "clustering" or "concentrating" in the recidivist group; (3) to analyze and interpret the concentration of isolated social characteristics relating to juvenile recidivism.

The following specific questions serve to delimit our focus of interest:

1. What are the social characteristics - age, residence and neighborhood, types of offenses, number of times repeated, other siblings referred to court, the parental status of parents, home adjustment, school adjustment, mental health and religious affiliations?
2. What is the marital status of parents, educational background, occupations and income?
3. What is the home lifestyle of family, size of family and housing accommodation? Hypotheses-that there is a high concentration of the social characteristics selected in this study, in the juvenile recidivist group.

Data and Method - The methods employed in this study are the stratified random sample and case study. The information collected in this study was obtained by studying the court records of each recidivist. by a questionnaire data sheet, interviews with recidivists, their parents, probation officers and other pertinent court personnel at Fulton County Justice Court, Atlanta, Georgia.

The writer, who has been employed at the court for over six (6) years as a probation officer and the past two (2) years as a probation officer supervisor, collected the data and information for the study.

Survey of Related Literature - The recidivist or repeater is one of the major problems in prevention and treatment of delinquency. Some authorities insist that only a juvenile who commits repeated delinquent acts should be termed a juvenile delinquent.

The literature relating to juvenile recidivism tends to indicate that there are precipitating social factors that surround those persons who persist in repeated acts of delinquency.

The most complete information on the relation of childhood background factors to recidivism is supplied by the Gluecks. One thousand delinquent boys who had passed through the juvenile court and the Judge Baker Foundation of Boston were studied at 5-year intervals until a total span of 15 years had passed from the time of their first examination.

One phase of the study compared the background characteristics of the men who reformed with the background of those who continued to recidivate. Certain characteristics were more closely associated with recidivism than with successful adjustment. Factors associated with recidivism than with successful adjustment. Factors associated with recidivism included poor discipline by the parents; mental disease or distortion; marked personality liabilities or unusual adolescent instability: truancy and other school misconduct; and one set of delinquent behavior in the preadolescent years.

In another study, the Gluecks traced 500 young male offenders who had been sentenced to the reformatory, from the time of discharge either unconditionally or from parole until a period of 15 years had passed. At the end of that time they were able to compare 140 reformed offenders with 256 recidivists. Family background factors more closely associated with recidivism than with reform were these: delinquency of other members of the family; low economic status of parents; employment of the mother outside the home; dependence of the family on welfare agencies; broken homes; incompatibility of parents. Characteristics of the offender in his prereformatory period that were more closely associated with recidivism than with reform were these: mental deficiency; mental pathology; truancy; first delinquency under the age of 14; first departure from home under the age of 14; ability to do only unskilled work; poor work habits; inability to meet economic responsibilities; and lack of affectionalties with parents and siblings.

In general, the factors in youth that were associated with continued delinquency and crime in adulthood centered around the home, the school, mental effect or instability, and work habits. The early family life of confirmed adult offenders appeared disorganized, involving conflict between the parents, low moral standards, poor discipline of the children, and often the absence of one parent. The economic standard was low, and the mother was possibly employed outside the home.

The Glueck studies revealed further that family ties were weak. At school, frequent factors were truancy, misconduct, and retardation, often linked with low mental ability. Delinquencies started during childhood. In adolescence, the delinquent tended to leave home and failed to learn either good work habits or a skill or trade.

The family's relationship to delinquency may be stated as follows as listed by Caven:*

1. Parents, because of personal and emotional difficulties of their own, are unable to give their children adequate personality training.
2. Parents, because of lack of education or unfamiliarity with the culture in which they live, may be unable to cope with destructive community forces.
3. Parents may be oriented to criminal behavior and find nothing wrong in condoning or actually training their children in similar patterns of attitude and behavior.
4. Men and women often come into marriage and become parents without having previously achieved maturity or an integrated personality. It is extremely difficult for such parents to assume the best parental roles toward their children. Louis Berlin, a probation officer with Kings County Court, Brooklyn, New York, during a surge of recidivism in his caseload, noted some basic similarities in the precipitating factors which suggested to him an explanation for recidivism.

The cases that suggested the explanation to him were those of teenagers, sixteen to nineteen years old, who live in residential sections of Queens, N.Y.C. They come from homes with middle-class values and ambitions. When the parents live together, the mother is usually the dominant, overprotective authority. According to Berlin, in some cases, where the parents were divorced or separated, the probationer usually lived with his mother, who is employed. Berlin's study indicated that practically all cases show some disturbance in family-child relationships. Further, their I.Q.'s range from the sixties to above average.

Berlin states that, "there is always a critical event which threatens the probationer's self-esteem or self-worth to precipitate his acting-out.

Tracing the dynamics of Violations of Probation, Berlin isolated four distinct links in the chain of phenomena as follows:

1. First, a stressful situation occurs in the life of the probationer which
2. devaluates his self-worth or ego-value which
3. arouses in the youth resentment and hostility toward the devaluator, and concomitant feelings of guilt and self-destructiveness which
4. the youth expresses in an anti-social act, a way which not only harms other persons or property but puts him in danger as well.

According to John W. Mannering in his study of recidivists, he indicates that the recidivist is more likely to come from blighted areas where privation and criminality prevail and criminal ways are more common than contracts with law-abiding forces.

Mannering states that "Recidivism studies generally reveal that certain types of offenses are more likely than others to be committed or repeated by recidivists. Larceny, burglary, robbery, car theft, and forgery are often cited as being the most recidivistic crimes. Homicide, assault, rape, other sex offenses, embezzlement, and income tax fraud are offenses not likely to be repeated.

It might be noted that Mannering's study consisted primarily of adult recidivists. However, Charles B. Thompson in a recidivist study found little correlation between age and recidivism and observed that, "recidivism is as much a function of youth as age.

Dr. David C. Twain in his current research related to crime and delinquency, relates the extent to which delinquency is associated with a huge range of socio-cultural factors and problems. The following paragraphs contain some of the highlights:

1. Findings regarding lower class child rearing practices indicate that these parents often fight uphill battles to guide and control their children in their debilitated communities and then collapse under the pressures that are destructive of proper parental functioning; that the relation of unemployment and men's reaction to this fact and to the disparagement of lower class men by their wives are probable factors in delinquency at this socio-economic status level.

2. Cross-cultural studies suggest that, among ethnic groups, it is not socio-economic disadvantages per se that promote delinquency, but a drift away from indigenous norms, group and family loyalties, and social rewards, resulting in a greater vulnerability to disadvantage.

3. Studies of adult urban Negro males have so far yielded the interesting result that their adolescent behavior or misbehavior seems better predicted by the stability and presence of their fathers than by socio-economic variables.

The high rate of recidivism for probationers and parolees tends to indicate that correctional institutions are limited in their efforts to reform and rehabilitate habitual offenders. The following statement might give some insight into the problem.

Modern investigations show that the inmate leaves without a marketable skill, with low reading and math levels, and returns to his former environment angrier at the world and himself than he was before his incarceration. His existence becomes one cycle after another through the revolving door.

Donald R. Taft, Professor Emeritus of Sociology, University of Illinois, maintains that the general culture has an influence on crime; and that there are criminogenic (crime-producing) aspects of the American society. In assessing the background of offenders, he relates that thousands of delinquents have lived in broken, strife-torn, or otherwise disorganized or inadequate homes.

The following excerpts give a description of the slum dwellers' plight.

They have lived in a neighborhood slum known and despised as a seedbed of crime and populated by a collection of life's discards whose relative poverty and degradation label them as failures in a period of great prosperity ...

The slum dweller may rebel or he may just accept his fate, too discouraged to object openly, and drifting into criminalistic patterns as the easiest reaction ...

American youth are dominated by their "desire to rate." Many young criminals have not been admitted to socially acceptable small primary groups and they join other associates and engage in activities which are in conflict with the larger society.

Dr. Taft states that the criminal has lived in a state of anomie with a relative absence of approved moral standards. Other offenders have been members of an underprivileged class or minority group where they have experienced discrimination, exploitation and frustration.

Dr. Taft enumerates the following examples of the criminogenic influence of certain aspects of American culture:

1. Belief that everyone has a racket.

2. Influence of destitution or relative poverty.

3. The search for something for nothing.

4. The influence of misrepresentation in advertising.

5. Preferential loyalties.

6. Influence of white-collar crime.

7. Growing acceptance of violence.

Dr. Dugald S. Arbuckle, Professor of Education at the Boston University School of Education and D. Lawrence Litwack, Assistant Professor, raised the following question in their study on Recidivism among Juvenile Delinquents:

Why does one boy, legally classified as a juvenile delinquent, and exposed to the rehabilitative measures of a state training school, return to his former illegal pursuits after parole, while another, with the same legal classification, and exposed to the same measures, succeeds while on parole and makes a satisfactory adjustment to society? What seems to be the characteristics that differentiate between the two of them and the groups they represent?

Their findings and conclusions concerning the above question indicated that few studies were found that distinguished between recidivists and non-recidivists from a prediction standpoint.

The implications of the Arbuckle and Litwack study is summarized in the following statement:

The success of a training school rehabilitative program can be measured only partially in terms of the rate of success among the parolees from the institution. Trying to judge the efficacy of an institution's program by the rate of success of its parolees fails to take into account the number of uncontrollable and indefinite factors that govern human conduct. The seeds of recidivism may be found within the psychological framework of the boy, within the practices of a training school, within the environment of the boy, or within the parole practices of any given state. The problem of insufficient staff, poorly trained personnel, overcrowded institutions, and overloaded parole agents merely serves to intensify the problems of recidivism.

Kirkpatrick found eight factors to have a bearing on recidivism. Examining only first offenders, he found the following to be relevant:

1. Age

2. Color

3. School problems

4. School grades

5. Number of Children in a family

6. Neighborhood

7. Type of offense

8. Number of Agencies in contact with family

It might be noted that Kirkpatrick's study is over 30 years old and he possibly did not have the benefit of the more recent findings in the area of urbanization, poverty, race and other economic and social factors.

In an article on the "Cultural Background of the Persistent Offender," Alexander Van West, explores some of the social dynamics surrounding the questions of who the recidivist is and where he comes from.

In examining the relationship between crime and social class, Dr. West points out that, "in Detroit, for example, 15 times as many criminals per unit of population came from a blighted area as from a normal residential area. In Jacksonville, Florida, the cost of police protection in underdeveloped areas was 12 times more per unit area than the remainder of the city.

One can go on almost indefinitely quoting statistics, sowing the correlation between substandard living conditions and the crime rate. This does not mean that these substandard conditions cause deviant behavior, for statisticians recognize that correlation does not imply causation.

The recidivists, for the most part, are the lower classes, the slum dwellers, and represent approximately 17 percent of the total population in our large cities according to West. He states further that of this group, approximately 52 per cent are considered semiskilled, while 46 per cent are unskilled and approximately 2 per cent have never worked at all. The jobs available to these people are usually low-paying, requiring long hours—6 or 7 days a week. West cites an example in Washington, D.C., concerning car washers who make 50¢ to 75¢ an hour and work 10½ hours a day, 6 and sometimes 7 days a week. Because of the low pay received by the men, the wives must also work. The following passage further illustrates their plight:

> Further analysis reveals that the lower class has the highest percentage of wives and mothers gainfully employed-approximately 48 percent. Most of them work at semiskilled factory jobs or are employed as maids, cleaning women, laundry women, and scrub women. A large percentage of the mothers employed have children between the ages of 6 and 16. Where the man alone works, the median income is approximately $2,600 per year. Where both husband and wife are employed, the median income is approximately $4,300 per year. Because of their lack of training and lack of available jobs which they can do, these people earn as much at 26 years as they do at age 45, and after 55 the income usually drops until the man or woman goes on relief. When hard times come, this is the first group of people to bear the brunt of any recession. Even if the inclination were there, low and inconsistent income preclude any planned saving systems. Monies must first be used for the necessities of life and when these are paid for there is very little, if anything, left over.

The above type of economic existence can easily lead to the philosophy. "live today for who knows what is going to happen tomorrow." *Get what you can now, satisfy your immediate needs, and to hell with the consequences," which is an attitude common among offenders.

In terms of education, Dr. West found that the median number of years of school is approximately 6 for the men and 8 for the women. Further, that 54 percent of the men and 39 percent of the women have less than a 7th grade education. Dr. West relates tests administered by himself in the District of Columbia to persons who have completed the 8th, 9th, or 10th grades, but who are reading at the 3rd, 4th or 5th grade level. Many of the teachers who teach in these schools, says Dr. West, have long since given up the idea of educating these students. These teachers are now a cross between policeman and entertainer. They try to keep the children entertained and interested and out of trouble.

Commenting about the families of the lower class and slum dwellers, Dr. West makes the following statement:

> Approximately 41 percent of children under 17 years of age live as a result of death, desertion, separation, or divorce. These families usually have mixed constellations which include a parent, children, roomers and/or boarders, common-law wives, husbands, by friends, etc. Desertion of the family by either the mother or the father is not uncommon and a good majority of the homes have three generations living in the same apartment. This conglomeration makes an excellent bed for pathology.

Sterling Tucker, Director, Field Services Department, National Urban League, Inc. gives some insight into some of the problems which face the ghetto dwellers. Tucker contends that the most serious of all criminal offenses occur with the greatest frequency in the slum areas of our largest cities. And, over 40 percent of the population of inner-city slums is black.

There are many, says Tucker, who juxtaposes facts and statistics thus in an effort to prove a relationship between race and the perpetration of crime, between blackness and criminality. However, neither race nor color—in and of itself is a factor that bears any relation whatsoever to the commission of crime according to Tucker. Rather, Numerous studies indicate that what matters is where in the city one is growing up, not religion or nationality or race.

It is no cliché that slums breed despair, hopelessness, degradation, disease of the body and disease of the mind. Slum areas are colorless, drab, and monotonous. There is little of beauty while examples of dilapidation and shabbiness abound. The slum dweller feels little pride as he looks around the outside or the inside of his home. Indeed, shame is the more common reaction... home has little holding power for the child—it is not physically pleasant or attractive; it is not a place to bring his friends; it is not even very much the reassuring gathering place of his own family....

A lack of space also characterizes the slum environment; there is not enough room for privacy; there but limited space for recreation and play. Space is always at a premium— inside or out; privacy and freedom are sought but in vain. Apartments or homes are shared with relatives or friends. Rooms are shared with brothers, sisters, cousins, parents.

Ghetto property, more often than not, is in a state of poor repair. Facilities are inadequate to meet the need ... plumbing and heating frequently fail; appliances are old and rickety and highly erratic. There are no traces of stability or permanence or durability to be found. Residents are forced to live with no assurances. The heating system may fail on the bitterest of winter evenings; rats may appear or reappear...

Slum neighborhoods team with criminal activity that is apparent to even the youngest pair of eyes. Dope pushers, numbers runners, prostitutes, pimps, and drunks are on the streets when the children leave for school in the morning; they are on the streets when children pass by again after class or after work. Bars are everywhere. Violence is part of the landscape. A sense of frustration and failure is in the air ... holding ghetto dwellers back is not a lack of will, but lack of opportunity. By following conventional routes, they can't get a good education, they can't get decent employment, they can't become upwardly mobile, they can't get out.

The foregoing description of the ghetto and the ghettoized seems to fit the definition phrased by Julius Horwitz, "A slum is a neighborhood where people infect one another with the virus of failure, and where children are infected long before the virus is detected.

It is apparent that the literature is replete with environmental conditions and social characteristics surrounding the whole area of crime, delinquency and recidivism. The most common and reoccurring social characteristics of juvenile recidivists seem to be related to the areas of poverty, blighted neighborhoods, broken homes, a lack of achievement and adjustment in school, inadequate care and supervision, a lack of healthy emotional and family ties.

Further summary and analysis of the literature on recidivism reveals that there is a gap between aspiration and opportunity. Because many delinquents and criminals are denied acceptance in the general mainstream of American society these persons have acquired certain social values and a general philosophy of life that is in conflict with the general society. The delinquent is bored; he is not at peace with himself; he is not at peace with society; he is not comfortable with his values; he is not comfortable with either the way he or the world is.

The crux of the delinquency problem seems to be related to the discrepancy between what adults teach children and what adults do themselves; a discrepancy between what adults believe and what they practice. The delinquent, sensing this confusion in values, the discrepancy between what is taught and what he experiences instinctively, seeks immediate gratification as a substitute for harmony. Once he seeks immediate gratification, the emphasis on long-range goals is lost.

Dr. Donald J. Tyrell makes the following statement concerning the groups from which delinquents are referred:

> It is interesting to note at this point that the family Court at Chicago in the past 10 years has not had one referral of an oriental child. In terms of the population in Cook County, there should have been approximately 100 such referrals

during this time. Jewish children are very seldom referred to the court. The great bulk of referrals are from Protestants and Catholic groups. Of these, the largest percent is from the Negro Protestant group.?

It seems apparent from the literature on juvenile recidivism and other related literature, that there is no single theory to describe it, However, there are some factors associated with juvenile recidivism. It is suspected that some of these factors surrounding recidivism will emerge in the study at Fulton County Juvenile Court.

CHAPTER 2
SOCIAL CHARACTERISTICS OF RECIDIVISTS

The social characteristics of juvenile recidivists cover a wide range. It is not the purpose of this chapter to attempt to include all of the social characteristics within this wide range. Also, many of these social factors can be applied to some juveniles who are not considered delinquents, and to some delinquents who have not been adjudged recidivists. However, it is suspected that when these social characteristics apply to the non-delinquents and the non-recidivists, it will be in isolated and individual cases. This chapter aims at examining those social characteristics that seem to be more commonly applied to juvenile recidivists referred to Fulton County Juvenile Court. It appears that these characteristics are more common to, and concentrated in the juvenile recidivist group. This chapter is concerned with an analysis of the following characteristics of the juvenile recidivist:

1. Age

2. Residence and Neighborhood Status

3. Types of Offenses

4. Number of Times Referred to Court

5. Other Siblings Referred to Court

6. Parental Status

7. Home Adjustment

8. School Adjustment

9. Mental Health

10. Religious Affiliation

Age—In Table 1, the present chronological ages of the recidivists are presented. There is no analysis in this study of the ages of the recidivists when they were first referred to the court. However, the dates covering their offenses and referrals to the court will be presented in this study. Age, as a residence, is a factor in determining jurisdiction of the court. The jurisdictional age varies from state to state. The Georgia Juvenile Court has original jurisdiction of persons under 17 years of age who are referred to the court as being in an apparent state of delinquency or dependency. The above age jurisdiction refers to the age of child at the time the child was found in a state of delinquency and/or dependency. Once the court gets jurisdiction, it can by court order, extend its services to the youngster until he reaches his 21st birthday. The Fulton County Juvenile Court seldom extends services to juveniles beyond their 18th birthday for various reasons.

Usually, children under 10 years of age when referred to the court fall in the category of "dependency" with allegations of neglect or a lack of supervision by parents. Children between the ages of 10 and 17 are the ones brought before the court and adjudicated as delinquent.

Table 1 indicates the highest percentage of recidivists, 57.5% are between 15 and 16 years of age, followed by the second highest percent, 27.5%. Twelve-point five percent are between the ages of 17 and 18. Only 2.5% fell between 11 and 12 years of age. The 15 and 16-year-old group account for slightly over half of the recidivists in the sample. 57.5%. followed by the 13 and 14-year-old group which consists of 27.5%. It is apparent that the low percent, 2.5% of the 11 and 12-year-old group is partly accounted for by the fact that this age group has had as much time to recidivate as the older groups. Secondly, a child must be at least 10 years of age (with few exceptions) before he is adjudicated delinquent by the court. Thirdly, the probation officers make every effort, especially on misdemeanor type offenses, to adjust or otherwise dispose of the case without a formal court hearing.

TABLE 1
AGE OF RECIDIVIST AT FULTON COUNTY JUVENILE

Age			Total	
		Number		Percent
17-18		5		12.5
15-16		23		57.3
13-14		11		27.5
11-12		1		2.5
Total		40		100.0

Residence and neighborhood - Where in Fulton County do the recidivists live? Generally, from what types of residence and from what neighborhood areas do they come? The samples indicate that no particular neighborhood is immune to delinquency and recidivism. However, none of the persons in the samples represented the upper class. There were about three individual cases in three neighborhoods that could be classified as middle class. However, only one municipality outside of the City of Atlanta was represented.

The sample indicates that there is a higher incidence of delinquency and recidivism in some neighborhoods than in others. There appears to be a higher concentration of recidivists in the lower socio-economic status neighborhoods than in the higher socio-economic status neighborhoods.

The 40 samples represented approximately 18 community areas in Metropolitan Atlanta. However, 75% of the samples fell in, roughly. 8 community areas with names and percentages as follows:

1. Summerhill (15%)

2. West End (15%)

3. Cabbage Town (10%)

4. Fourth Ward (7.5%)

5. Perry Homes Area (7.5%)

6. Pittsburgh (7.5%)

7. Vine City (7.5%)

8. Dixie Hills (5%)

It might also be noted that 11 recidivists or 27.2% live in low-rent Government Housing Projects. Also, many of the recidivists live in the Model Cities Area of the city.

The recidivists seem to be more highly concentrated in the Atlanta Metropolitan Area in the lower socio-economic neighborhoods predominantly populated by Negroes. These neighborhoods seem to be characterized by a conglomeration of low-rent apartment dwellings, and unstable and deteriorating housing, with numerous businesses and other public concerns. With the crowded conditions, there seems to be a lack of space and facilities for wholesome recreation.

Twenty-one or 52.5% of the recidivists live in apartments. Eighty percent of the homes where recidivists live are rented. The average rent is $66.50 per month. Eight or 20% of the houses where recidivists live are owned or being bought.

The homes where the recidivists live consist of an average of 4½ rooms. An average of 6 persons live in these homes.

The mobility and number of times the recidivists and their families relocated were not a factor for analysis in this study. However, it was noted from the recidivists' records that they relocate frequently, primarily within the same class of neighborhoods.

Type of offenses -The 40 recidivists committed a total of 316 offenses beginning at the first offense in December 1962 through June 1970. Each recidivist has been referred to the court on an average of 8 times. This does not include multiple offenses. In many instances, a juvenile is arrested for burglary, and the investigation later reveals that he committed several burglaries or other offenses. Therefore, the total number of 316 more accurately gives the number of times the juveniles were referred to the court and not an accurate number of the offenses. The total number 316 can be safely used as a conservative estimate. Also, the total number 316 does not include traffic offenses. Traffic offenses are not considered to be in the delinquent category unless they are of a substantially serious nature or habitually repeated by the same juvenile.

As Table 2 indicates, there are 11 different offenses with relatively high frequencies. Thefts, Burglary, Auto theft, Acts of Malicious Mischief, Ungovernability, Shoplifting, Violation of Compulsory School Attendance Law, Drinking or possessing Alcoholic Beverages, Running away or Escape, Glue Sniffing and Injury to persons, are the most frequently occurring offenses. The other 8 classes of offenses were committed less than 10 times.

Many, if not most of the 316 offenses were adjusted or disposed of without a formal court hearing. Many of the juveniles had committed several offenses over a period of years before they were taken to court and adjudicated delinquent. All of the 27 Probationers of this sample were found delinquent by the court and placed on probation in 1969. In order to be considered recidivists, all of the probationers have committed additional acts of delinquency since they were placed on Probation in 1969.

The 13 parolees used in the sample, likewise have committed several or many offenses before being found delinquent and sent to the Youth Development Center. Most of the parolees had their probation revoked before being committed to the Youth Development Center. However, each parolee was placed on parole in 1969 and has committed a subsequent act or several subsequent acts of delinquency.

This research is not a comparative study and race is not used as a factor for analysis. However, Table 3, shows the number of times the recidivists repeated acts of delinquency for the 28 Negro samples and the 12 white samples.

TABLE 2
DELINQUENT COMPLAINTS OF FORTY RECIDIVISTS
FROM DECEMBER 1962-JUNE 1970

Complaints (Offenses)	Frequency
Automobile Theft	43
Burglary	44
Attempted Burglary	4
Robbery	4
Other Thefts	45
Violations of Compulsory School Attendance Law	22
Ungovernable	12
Sex Offense	1
Injury to Person (Assault and Battery)	11
Acts of Malicious Mischief	32
Drinking or Possessing Alcoholic Beverages	12
Arson	1
Gambling	1
Possessing and/or using Dangerous Weapons	7
Violation of Curfew Ordinance	8
Violation of Probation and Parole	4
Glue Sniffing	10
Shoplifting	26
Violation of States Narcotics Law	2
Total	316

The above complaints do not include traffic offenses. Siblings referred to court. Twenty-five or 62.5 percent of the recidivists had other siblings who had also been referred to court for delinquent offenses. Twelve or 30 percent of the recidivists had 1 sibling referred to court. Seven or 17.5

percent of the recidivists had two siblings who were referred to juvenile court. Three or 7.5 percent of the recidivists had 3 siblings who were referred to court. Three or 7.5 percent of the recidivists had 4 siblings who were referred to court. With the exception of two cases, the siblings were boys.

Most of the other siblings were older, and many had passed the age of Juvenile Court jurisdiction. They had committed in most instances, the same, or similar offenses.

TABLE 3
NUMBER OF TIMES JUVENILE RECIDIVISTS
REPEATED ACTS OF DELINQUENCY

Number of Times Repeated	Negro Boys (Frequency)	White Boys (Frequency)
1	0	0
2	1	0
3	4	2
4	3	1
5	1	2
6	6	1
7	4	2
8	2	2
9	0	1
10	2	0
11	2	1
12	1	0
13	2	0
Total	28	12

Parental status of Recidivists Parents.-The highest percentage of the recidivists lived with one parent, the mother. Living with the "mother only" category accounts for over half of the sample, which is more than all of the other categories where the child was living when referred to the Court combined.

The next highest percentage category of the whereabouts of the child, when referred to the Court, is with both parents, which accounted for less than half the number living with the mother.

These two categories combined, account for 77 percent of the sample. The remaining 23 percent live with foster parents, father, cousin, aunt, sister and self as indicated in Table 4.

TABLE 4
WHEREABOUTS OF CHILD WHEN REFERRED TO THE COURT

Lives with	Number	Percent
Mother Only	21	52.0
Both Own Parents	10	25.0
Father Only	2	5.0
Foster Parents	2	5.0
Aunt	1	2.5
Sister	1	2.5
Brother	1	2.5
Cousin	1	2.5
Self	1	2.5
Total	40	100.0

Table 4 seems to indicate that when the mother and father are living apart, the probability that the juvenile will live with the mother is greatest. Considering that the juvenile is living with his mother when the mother and father are living apart in 52.5 percent of the cases, and also with the mother when both parents are living together in 25 percent of the cases, indicates that the mother lives in the home with the recidivist in 77.5 percent of the cases.

By contrast the percentage of cases in the recidivist lives with his father when the parents live apart and when they are living together, it is found to be 5 percent and 25 percent respectively.

Therefore, when recidivists' parents are living apart, the probability of the child living with the father is slight. Combining the two percentages with parents together and apart the father is in the home with the child in 5 percent of the cases compared to the mother's 52 percent of the cases; 30 percent of the cases compared to the mother's 77 percent of the cases.

In three of the cases, there were indications that the maternal grandmother lived in the home with the mother when the father was away.

Two cases where the father was away indicated stepfathers in the home. However, the marital status of these step-fathers was not clear.

<u>Home adjustment</u> - There are frequent and consistent indications from the recidivists' court records and from interviews with them and their parents, that most of them have extremely unhappy home situations. The recidivist often expresses rebellion and hostility towards his parents and other authoritative figures.

Thirty out of 40 of the recidivists were referred to Court for being ungovernable, running away from home or for some other severe conflict with their parents. Seventy-five percent of the recidivists have problems growing out of their home and parental relationships.

In many instances, if not most, the parents are inadequate and have insufficient resources to cope with their own problems, not to mention the child's problem.

The above paragraph will be better understood as the parents of recidivists are treated in the next chapter.

School adjustment - A school problem seems to be one of the most constant characteristics of recidivists. The sample does not indicate a single successful student in school. Fifteen, or 37.5 percent of the recidivists were found to have disturbing and disrupting behavior at school, in addition to excessive absences and failures in-class work. Eleven, or 27.5 percent, were found to have excessive unexcused absences and chronic truant problems. There were indications showing that 85 percent of the recidivists had definite problems in school; ranging from cutting classes, excessive unexcused absences, truancy, and disruptive behavior to incorrigibility.

There were 2 out of 40 recidivists with no indications that they were serious school problems. Four recidivists assumed to have dropped out of school had no indications of school adjustment.

Table 5 indicates the schools where recidivists were enrolled during the second semester of the 1969-70 school year. Table 6 indicates the grades of the recidivists.

Over ninety percent are underachievers in school Many are retarded, functionally illiterate and cannot read.

TABLE 5
SCHOOLS WHERE RECIDIVISTS WERE ENROLLED THE
SECOND SEMESTER 1969-70 SCHOOL YEAR

Schools	Recidivists
Archer H.S.	1
Brown H.S.	3
Bryant H.S.	1
Carver H.S.	2
Central H.S.	4
Douglas H.S.	2
Fulton (S) H.S.	1
Fulton (W) H.S.	1
Grady H.S	1
Harper H.S.	1
Hope H.S.	1
Howard H.S.	3
Northside H.S	1
Price H.S	1
Pitts H.S	1
Parks Jr. H.S.	1
Russell H.S. (East Point)	1
Roosevelt H.S.	3
Sylvan H.S.	1
Spring Street E.S.	1
Smith H.S.	2
Slaton E.S.	1
Scott E.S.	1
Washington H.S.	2
None	3
Total	40

H. S.-High School: E. S.-Elementary School

TABLE 6
SCHOOL GRADES OF RECIDIVISTS

School Grade	Number	Percent
12th	2	5.0
11th	3	7.5
10th	3	7.5
9th	8	20.0
8th	12	30.0
7th	1	2.5
6th	4	10.0
5th	1	2.5
EMR	1	2.5
None Given	5	12.5
Total	40	100.0

*Mean grade is 8th.

Mental Health - Fifteen or 37.5 percent of the recidivists were referred to the Mental Health Clinic at the Juvenile Court. The diagnoses reveal that most of their intelligence quotients (IQs) measure under 90. The psychological and psychiatric reports frequently indicate defective character structure because of a disturbed home; rejected by parents; resentful and hostile towards mother; poor self-concept and image; no masculine authority figure in the home; confused and frustrated; spoiled and indulged by grandparents; broken homes; unstable mothers and deserted fathers. To mention an extreme example, one recidivist along with two younger siblings, was born in prison while the mother was doing a life sentence for murder.

Religious Affiliation - The highest percent of the recidivism claimed affiliation with a Baptist Church. Sixty-two percent of the recidivists along with their parents, made the claim of being affiliated with a Baptist church. Ten or 25 percent made no claim of religious affiliation. The other religious groups represented were as follows: Methodists 2 or 5 percent; Presbyterians 1 or 2.5 percent; Holiness 1 or 2.5 percent; Jewish 1 or 2.5 percent.

Most of the recidivists have no recent church attendance. A few indicated that they attend church occasionally. It can be concluded from the recidivists' records and from interviews with them and their parents that religion played no significant role in their lives.

TABLE 7
RECIDIVISTS' CLAIMS OF RELIGIOUS AFFILIATION

Religious Affiliation	Number	Percent
Baptist	25	62.5
Methodist	2	5.0
Presbyterian	1	2.5
Holiness	1	2.5
Jewish	1	2.5
None Claimed	10	25.0
Total	40	100.0

CHAPTER 3
THE PARENTS AND HOME ENVIRONMENT OF RECIDIVISTS

Marital status of parenting - The varied marital statuses of the recidivists' parents are suggestive of marital conflicts, confusion, embarrassment, instability and disharmony in the family. It is not uncommon to find a high percentage of unmarried mothers with large numbers of children fathered by many different putative fathers. It is not uncommon for a delinquent recidivist to not know who his father is. There is often no contact between the child and the putative father.

It is not uncommon for putative fathers to deny being the father of many delinquents. It is recognized that this kind of situation is not limited to delinquents and recidivists. However, because of the high rate of parents who never married, separated, deserted by their father, divorced and living separately or alone for other reasons, it is suspected that the recidivists have a higher concentration of those unfortunate marital conflicts and broken home situations.

The sample indicated that 13 or 32 percent of the recidivists' parents were separated; 10 or 25 percent were never married; three or 7.5 percent were widowed.

The 8 or 20 percent that were married gave indications that there was a lack of harmony in the home. There were reports of drinking problems, temporary separations, a lack and mismanagement of money, long hours away from home and a lack of congenial love and consideration between the spouses.

Table 8 gives the varied marital statuses of recidivists' parents.

TABLE 8
MARITAL STATUS OF RECIDIVISTS' PARENTS

Marital Status	Number	Percent
Married	8	20.0
Never Married	10	25.0
Separated	13	32.5
Divorced	2	5.0
Widowed	3	7.5
Widowered	2	5.0
Unknown	2	5.0
Total	40	100.0

Home life style of family - Interviews with the recidivists and their parents concerning their home life indicate that the children are often left unsupervised. The children, including the recidivists, wander through the neighborhoods and play in and outside of each other's homes with the benefit of little, if any, adult guidance and supervision. It is difficult to determine, but it appears that the family relationships are often tense and antagonistic. It seems that time, resources, family circumstances and estranged relationships don't permit many, if any, meaningful and enjoyable family experiences together.

The home life seems to be characterized generally, by disorganization, a lack of planning, indifference on the part of parents to set long-range meaningful goals for educational, social and economic betterment and progress.

Education of parents - The sample indicated that two parents, a mother and a father, finished high school. The same father also finished a business school. These two represented the highest known educational achievement among the parents.

Because of the large number of fathers living away from the home with the child, the educational background of 18 or 45 percent of the fathers could not be determined. One father had no formal education, 5 had less than a seventh-grade education; 15 had less than a twelfth-grade education.

The education of the mother followed a pattern similar to the father. Twenty mothers had less than a twelfth-grade education; 12 had less than a sixth-grade education; 7 were indicated as unknown.

From the indications in the Court records and from the questionnaire and interviews, the parents also have a background of poverty. Therefore, in all probability, they have substantially far less education than is indicated by their highest completed grades.

Occupation and income of parents - The range of occupations clearly indicates that none of the parents are professionally employed. Most of the known occupations, with few exceptions, indicate that these parents have few marketable skills. Most of them are employed in common labor and nonskilled jobs. As has been the case throughout this research, the information on the fathers is limited because of the high frequency of their being away from the home and generally unavailable. It is noted that the occupational and income status of 17 or 42.5 percent are unknown.

Table 9 gives an indication of the various occupations, disabilities and incapacities of the mother and father of the recidivists.

Most of these families appear to be economically dependent. Fifteen or 37.5 percent are receiving welfare assistance from the Division of Family and Children Services.

The average annual income of these families from all visible sources, including welfare, pensions, disability checks, money paid through Court for non-supporting fathers and earnings of parents amounted to $4200.

When one considers an average number of 6 people living in each home, the $4200 figure is further deflated. However, it is possible that some might be received by the family from such invisible sources or unreported income as relatives and friends.

The occupations, disabilities and incapacities listed in Table 9 further illustrate some of the background reasons why the recidivists have such a large number of broken homes, disorganized living patterns and disruptive home situations. It also explains, in part, why the recidivists are often misguided, unsupervised, unmotivated, uninspired and undisciplined. They have a combination of some of the most inadequate, uneducated, disabled, unfit, economically dependent, socially and culturally disadvantaged parents in the community. There is also a high percentage of deceased parents and an extraordinary number of parents, and especially fathers, away from the home of their children without any support or meaningful contact.

Living under the deprived conditions as stated above, the limited number of available parents do not often have adequate time or resources to meet or have met, the many needs of themselves and their children. Thus, it seems that the recidivist group has a concentration of negative social characteristics in their environment, which are conducive to a pathological breeding ground.

TABLE 9
OCCUPATIONS, DISABILITIES AND INCAPACITIES OF PARENTS

Father		Mother	
Occupations Disabilities Incapacities	Frequencies	Occupations Disabilities Incapacities	Frequencies
Unknown	17	Maid	10
Deceased	5	Unemployed	7
Disable	4	Deceased	3
Custodian	2	Cafeteria	3
Alcoholic	1	Laundry	3
Cosmetic Salesman	1	Nurses Aid	2
Bakery	1	Meat Co.	2
Retired	1	Unknown	2
Ford Plant	1	Scripto	1
Construction	1	Factory	1
Delivery Truck	1	Artist	1
Mechanic	1	Disable	1
Mental Hospital (Patient)	1	Egg Co.	1
Blue Collar	1	Voc. Rehab.	1
Steel Co.	1	Electric Co.	1
Painter			
Total	40	Total	40

Housing accommodation and size of family - According to the sample, over half of the recidivists live in four-room apartments with an average number of 6 persons living in the apartment. By adding the rooms of the 18 houses and the rooms of the 21 apartments, gives an average of four and one-half rooms for each family. There was no significant difference in the number of persons reported to have been living in the houses. Considering that two of the rooms are generally used for the kitchen and living room, it would seem that the homes are relatively crowded.

There are indications that the recidivist's home is often shared with relatives of both sexes and various ages. The recidivist's family also consists of both sexes and various ages which increase the need for more room and privacy.

There is not only a lack of physical space, but a lack of social space as well. The recidivist cannot always "turn off" or escape what he considers the unpleasant chatter, the constant nagging and the old-fashioned lectures by his parents. Many of the recidivists appear to be the "scapegoat" of the family and often gets more than their share of the blame and punishment. With such limited space to accommodate such a large number of people, hardly anyone, and especially the recidivist, can claim a room, a chair, a bed, or anything in the home that will be preserved for his own personal and private use. Consequently, the four or five rooms become too inhibitive, repressive and intimidating for the recidivist. This, among other reasons, could possibly contribute to the high percentage of running away from home and being ungovernable. If there are sufficient physical and social space in the recidivists home environment for him to escape some of these things which are unpleasant and threatening to him, he might not seek the many harmful and unlawful means of escape outside the home which result in repeated acts of delinquency.

CHAPTER 4
SUMMARY AND CONCLUSIONS

The findings in this study seem to be consistently conclusive from the data presented and analyzed that there are certain social characteristics that are common to, and highly concentrated in the juvenile recidivist group. It is acknowledged that many of the analyzed social characteristics have some degree of commonality with other similar groups. However, it is doubtful that such a high percentage of negative and unfavorable social characteristics are concentrated in the general delinquent population. As a probation officer with six years experience, the writer, having had numerous contacts with delinquent children, and their parents, and having familiarity with their social environment was nevertheless amazed at the large number of recidivists living under such unfavorable conditions- conditions which are not only unfavorable but also inimical to the natural processes of wholesome and healthy growth and development.

Basic findings.-The following list indicates the basic findings relating to the recidivists:

1. The majority of the recidivists are between 15 and 16 years of age.
2. With few exceptions, most of the recidivists live in low socioeconomic status neighborhoods.
3. General thefts, burglary, automobile theft, acts of malicious mischief, shoplifting, violation of the Compulsory School Attendance Law, ungovernability and glue sniffing were the most frequent offenses.

4. Each recidivist was referred to the court on an average of seven times each from December 1962 through June 1970.

5. Twenty-five of the forty recidivists had other siblings who had also been referred to the court with the number of siblings per recidivists, ranging from one to four.

6. The highest number of recidivists live with one parent, the mother. Living with the "mother only" category accounts for over half of the sample.

7. The study revealed that most of the recidivists were poorly adjusted at home. Thirty of the forty recidivists were often uncontrollable by their parents.

8. A school problem was found to be one of the most constant characteristics of the recidivist.

9. Fifteen of the recidivists had been referred to the Mental Health Clinic at the Juvenile Court.

10. Of the reported religious affiliations, most were Protestants with a high concentration of the Baptist denomination. Religion seems to play a very minor role in the lives of the recidivists.

The following list indicates the basic findings relating to the parents and home environment of the recidivists:

1. The marital status of the recidivists' parents were varied However, the highest number were separated, followed by those who never married These two categories accounted for over half of the marital statuses.

2. The home life style of the recidivists indicate that there is a lack of family cohesion and harmony The

parents are frequently away and the children are unsupervised.

3. Only two parents reported in the sample completed high school Twelve of the mothers had less than a sixth-grade education and five of the reported educational backgrounds of the fathers had less than a sixth-grade education.

4. The range of occupations ranged from unskilled to semiskilled type jobs Fifteen of the families were receiving welfare assistance There were a large number of non— non-supporting fathers Forty-two hundred dollars is the average family income.

5. According to the sample, over half of the recidivists live in four-room apartments with an average of six persons living in the apartment.

While it cannot be concluded that these social characteristics are causes of delinquency and recidivism, or that a plausible theory could be based on them, the analyzed data seem to give evidence that in some way, these social characteristics are contributing factors to be considered with the utmost concern.

It seems that the findings will support the generalization that recidivism is a potentiality at the core of delinquency and that to the extent that unfavorable social environmental conditions are concentrated in the recidivist group, recidivism is predictable in the delinquency population. This being the case, it would seem to indicate that recidivism will be, or can be, reduced in proportion to the reduction of the unfavorable environmental and social factors that will contribute to delinquency. Consequently, the core of the delinquency problem will begin to dissolve if such an approach is adopted.

There are several factors that stand out very conspicuously in this study. First is the observation that in this population are an unusual incredible number of children living apart from their fathers. The influence of this single factor may be an excuse of decisive influence on the development of the recidivist. The number of fathers being away from the home and the number of broken homes reported seem to suggest that such attention, planning and preparation must be given to the planning of the family structure. Secondly, poverty and its many ramifications also are revealed as a major factor in recidivism. This factor is highlighted and reinforced by the fact that most of the recidivism is concentrated in the inner core or outer city sections of Metropolitan areas where there are constant reminders of wealth and affluence. It was not surprising that the greatest number of recidivists came from impoverished neighborhoods. This seems to add strength to the theory that the environment gets into the person, and that culture is a dominant influence on a person's behavior. Thirdly, the fact that an overwhelming majority of the recidivists lack self-control would seem to suggest that there is a serious breakdown in the parent-child social relationships which is detrimental to all concerned-the child, the parents and society. A high percentage of this behavior extends into the school system also. It seems that our institutions must give more attention to character building and instilling more ethical and social values in human relations that are more positive and socially acceptable. The fourth outstanding factor was that religion did not seem to have any influence or place in the lives of the recidivists.

Future programs for rehabilitating and treating delinquency and recidivism must not be geared to the individual approach alone.

Future programs must also include working with the whole child, the whole family, and the whole community. They must be aimed at rebuilding impoverished neighborhoods and enriching fertile soil.

PART TWO

A FRAMEWORK FOR ESTABLISHING A COMMUNITY OUTREACH SOCIAL SERVICE PROGRAM

CHAPTER 5
INTRODUCTION

The ideas and development of this thesis are based on the writer's personal experience as a Community Outreach Supervisor and as Project Director-Correction Specialist of a four-year Outreach Program at Fulton County Juvenile Court in Atlanta, Georgia. The writer became the first Community Outreach Supervisor at the Court in 1971. Based on this initial Outreach Program the Law Enforcement Assistance Administration (LEAA) funded a one-million-dollar two-year Probation Outreach Project.

The LEAA-funded Project consisted of fifty professional and paraprofessional employees. Twelve community-based outreach offices were established throughout the high-crime communities in Atlanta. Approximately 400 official clients participated. Several thousand additional clients were referred to the Outreach Project and received short-term counseling, referral and supportive services.

There was very little published information available that could be used in the planning for community-based corrections or social services. The writer as Project Director, used a variety of sources and resources to establish and implement the Outreach Program.

Research was conducted in the areas of community-based social services and corrections at the beginning of the federally funded project in 1973. No significant work could be found as a guide in establishing a community-based social service program.

The Community Outreach Project at Fulton County Juvenile Court was the first of its kind in the Nation to succeed according to representatives of Atlanta Regional Commission and the Law Enforcement Assistance Administration. A precedent was set in Georgia by the establishment of the community-based Outreach Project at Fulton County Juvenile Court from 1973 to 1975.

This thesis is based on knowledge gained through personal experience in establishing, implementing and directing the previously described Outreach Program while serving in the capacity of Project Director. In addition to the four years of direct experience in community-based outreach social services, the writer has been a community worker for seven years as a Probation Officer and one year as a Director of a YMCA in a low socio-economic status neighborhood. A total of twelve years of professional experience in community social services goes into the preparation of this thesis.

The Economic Opportunity Act, Omnibus Crime Control And Safe Streets Act, The Juvenile Delinquency and Prevention Act and other recent anti-crime and anti-poverty related legislation and programs have contributed to a great emphasis on community-based outreach social services. Community-based services are being used in Georgia and other states to alleviate overcrowded prisons and other detention facilities. The Social Security Administration, Department of Health, Education and Welfare and other federal and local agencies are decentralizing their services into community-based offices.

This thesis will add to the areas of knowledge on how to establish, administer and operate community-based outreach social service programs. Most of the literature comes from the criminal justice area. However it is not intended to be limited to criminal justice programs. It is purposely designed to be a general framework and guideline for the establishment and operation of a wide variety of community social service programs. This is an approach used by David Easton. He presented a general framework that would encompass a variety of systems. The general concepts promulgated in this work are construed broadly for wide application. A specific program model would be less useful because of its limiting application in the presence of a wide variety of social service programs. The other contribution of this work is its rationale for community-based outreach services, which contains the essence and foundation for such services.

Community-based services and outreach services are terms used interchangeably in this thesis. Both are used to avoid the possible limited separate meaning of each. A community-based office does not necessarily have an outreach component. Its services might be limited to the confines of the office. On the other hand, an outreach program does not necessarily have a community-based office. The outreach workers could conceivably operate from an office outside the community in this instance. The preceding examples of community-based services and outreach services indicate two different meanings. Community service programs can be based on either or both concepts.

The complete concept this thesis seeks to describe is community-based outreach social services where there is an office located in the community out of which there are mobile community workers extending services to the residents in a personal manner.

As used in this paper the term community refers to, "a body of people, their organizations, and their ways of working together to provide or regulate a network of basic services." A community and municipality are often linked together in the public's mind (and even occasionally in the dictionary), but the two are distinctly different according to Greenberg. 28 He explains that a community is defined in social terms and a municipality is defined in legal terms.

A review of the limited literature on community-based services did not reveal the internal mechanics of establishing and operating a community outreach office. The function of management in the literature of the various programs is not explored. Management is an important factor in the operation of most if not all, social service programs. It is especially important in the operation of community-based programs because of the wide distribution of staff throughout the community. The difficulty of management increases with the dispersion of staff. The significance of management is summarized in the following statement:

Management, we have said, is the determiner of our economic progress, the employer of our educated, the amasser of our resources, the strength of our national defense, and the molder of our society. It is the core of all our public as well as personal activities. And it is all these things because man has found no substitute for it in the effective achievement of his goals.

Most of the literature gave an outside view and an examination of the results of particular outreach programs. It was not the purpose of the literature examined to give guidance on the process and steps involved in setting up a community program or to provide the intimate details involved in its managerial operation.

There are no discernible attempts in the literature to examine the many components of a community-based program from an inside point of view. The community-based programs treated in the literature appear as one functional unit. The many entities of "nuts and bolts" that constitute a community-based program are not examined in the literature. The literature is geared primarily toward what the community program does and the purpose of its establishment. There is very little information on what the program itself constitutes. There was no composite information in the literature sufficient to be used as a model for structuring a community-based outreach social service operation.

Community-based outreach programs do not originate, exist, or operate in a vacuum. The literature examined does not discuss the political and social dynamics involved in the establishment and operation of community-based programs. The expertise, resources, knowledge and personnel used in setting up a community-based program will be a determining factor in its success. They will determine the quality of services provided. The literature contains a fair amount of discussion on the purpose and accomplishments of community programs. These are important studies of community programs. However, there is a lack of information on the structure and model of a community-based program.

The literature reflects an almost ninety-year history of the concept of community-based social services. One of the earliest concepts of community-based service was implemented by America's most distinguished social worker, Jane Addams. Jane Addams founded Hull House in a poor district of Chicago in 1889.0 According to Morton and Lucia White the task of Hull House Settlement was to remove hollowness or the void found in the lives of many people by reconstructing localism, by building within the city's small centers of neighborly communication to take up some of the void created by urban expansion.

Most of the programs initiated at Hull House illustrated Jane Addams's desire to recapture a sense of community and communication and to stimulate the exercise of natural powers that had been dammed up by life under conditions of urban poverty.

Walter C. Reckless cites studies that were done in the 1930s in Chicago regarding the treatment of delinquents in their communities. According to Reckless, Claude D. Shaw and Henry D. McKay conducted many community studies in relationship to crime and delinquency. Such studies contributed to the present emphasis on community-based treatment programs.

There have been a number of community projects in a number of cities, such as Synanon House in California, the Midcity Delinquency Control Project of New York City and the Chicago Area Projects that resulted from Shaw's and McKay's studies in the 1930's. There have been similar projects in other cities. Additionally, there have been many halfway houses, multi-purpose centers and other community centers of various descriptions. The trend towards community-based outreach social services appears to have started a significant increase in the 1960s and 1970s.

The general purpose and justification for community-based services are contained in the following quotations:

The general purpose of the neighborhood center is to serve as a spatial organizational focal point for grass-roots participation in self-help programs by the area residents.

The alienation and dehumanization engendered in jails, work-houses, prisons, even probation services, are to be avoided where possible. The less penetration into the criminal justice system the better.

Robert M. Carter expresses the idea that the movement toward community-based corrections is a move away from society's most ancient responses to those who violate the criminal code. For thousands of years, society relied mainly on banishment, physical punishment, or the death penalty to accomplish its goals of criminal justice. Out of the realization that the old ways were unacceptable, there emerged the prison, a place that Carter calls, "artificial banishment," or "civil death." After two centuries of experience with the penitentiary, we are beginning to realize that its benefits are transient at best.

According to Griggs and McCune, the period of greatest growth in community treatment programs was between 1968 and 1969, when six states implemented programs during each of those years.3 Griggs and McCune sent 50 questionnaires to each state department of corrections. Forty-six out of fifty (50) responded. According to their report, twenty-eight of the 46 departments (59 percent) had community treatment programs.

The study revealed that many types and combinations of physical facilities were used by states in operating their community treatment programs as follows:

Eight states used noncorrectional facilities only, such as hotels, YMCAs, apartments, etc. Five used state correctional institutions only. One used county jails only. Two used a combination of state correctional institutions and county jails. Six used a combination of state correctional institutions and noncorrectional facilities. Three used county jails and noncorrectional facilities. And three used a combination of county jails, state correctional institutions and noncorrectional facilities.

This study was limited to adult felons, male and female, who were programmed in the community before release or parole according to Griggs and McCune.

Information concerning many of the community-based programs that started in 1968 is beginning to find its way into print. Community-based programs take various diversionary forms. Some are designed to divert individuals from the criminal justice system such as the youth service bureaus. There are also police-level, pretrial and postconviction-level diversions. "If true diversion occurs, the individual is clearly placed outside of the official realm of the justice system and is immune from receiving any of the system labels.

The Probationed Offenders Rehabilitation and Training (PORT) Project of Olmsted County (Rochester, Minnesota) is one example of a community-based, residential program for convicted felons and adjudicated delinquents which aims at diverting offenders from the more traditional state prison, reformatory, and delinquency institutions.8 PORT is operated as a private, non-profit corporation under a board of directors composed of lay citizens, representatives of the local criminal justice system and supportive community agencies. This program is said to provide the court with an open residential facility as an alternative resource to State institution commitment; both adult and juvenile offenders who might otherwise be incarcerated in state institutions are diverted into the program. Discretion in the decision to divert to the PORT program is exercised by both the court and the program management.

The article by Joe Hudson and others, as well as an earlier article by Kenneth F. Schoen, indicates that PORT is a successful diversionary program.

The California Youth Authority has been conducting a large-scale, two-part experiment known as the Community Treatment Project (CTP). The first phase of the Project, 1961-1969 was carried out mainly in Sacramento and Stockton, with San Francisco being added in 1965.

The Community Treatment Project made it possible to compare the performance of youths who were placed directly in the intensive CTP program, without any prior institutionalization, against the performance of youths who were sent to an institution for several months before being returned to their home communities and then being given routine supervision within standard-sized parole caseloads. The second phase of CTP was conducted from 1969 to 1974. The primary objective was to try to determine if any of the youths in the experiment would become less delinquently oriented if they began their California Youth Authority career within a certain kind of residential setting, and not within the community itself.

A variety of community-based social service programs are being implemented in the United States and also in England and Wales.43 The Government of England promoted the Criminal Justice Act, of 1972, which has a provision aimed at strengthening the suspended sentence by adding, in certain cases, a requirement of supervision by a probation officer.* Along with the increase of community-based programs, there is also an emphasis on community involvement by volunteers. It is becoming more common to find volunteer organizations working with various social service programs in both, the institutional and community settings. In England, volunteers serve in over a thousand different projects throughout the country according to Clementine L. Kaufman.' "They are working in general and psychiatric hospitals, children's nurseries, and special schools for retardants, with immigrants, in institutions for the old or disabled, in delinquent institutions, and in community-based organizations.

The effectiveness of community-based programs is summed up by Joe Hudson as follows:

At the same time, while we may wish to believe that programs labeled as "diversionary" or "community-based" are more effective in achieving the desired result of rehabilitation, little reliable evidence can be produced in support of this belief. That such programs may be more humane, more economical, and do no worse than their conventional alternatives is justification enough for their continued support and expansion.

The purpose of this thesis is to provide a general framework for the establishment and operation of a community-based social service program that will serve to enhance the managerial functioning of such a program. Although most of the literature reviewed relates to criminal justice or correctional programs, the framework of this thesis is intended to apply to other types of social service or human service community-based programs as well.

CHAPTER 6
RATIONALE FOR COMMUNITY OUTREACH SERVICES

The primary purpose of a community outreach social service program is to provide services to the client as close as possible to the client's living environment. The presumption is that a client's problems and needs can be more effectively assessed and met from a personal knowledge of his living conditions and environment. Frequently, a close personal observation of a client's home life and community reveals some of the things that contributed to the client's problems. The vantage point of the community enables the outreach worker to get a more balanced picture of the kind of environment the client lives in and how the client relates to it. Therefore, a more informed and intelligent decision can be made regarding social service delivery.

The community setting provides more concrete information on which to base a plan for helping the client. The traditional way of working with a client is to require the client to report to the worker's office, which is usually far removed from the residence and community of the client. This method isolates the client from his living environment. The client does not usually communicate an accurate picture of his environment and problems. At best, it is hearsay information. In many instances, clients do not report to the worker's office but are contacted by telephone. Some workers never see the client or the community. It may not be necessary in all cases. However, community-based outreach services are intended to intensify social service delivery. They recognize the fact that human beings do not live in a vacuum, but live in diverse communities of various homogeneous and heterogeneous social relationships.

An outreach worker who is located in the community is in a position to observe, firsthand, the quality of life over a period of time. This cannot be done by sporadic visits to the community. The outreach worker who spends time in the community communicating with the residents is in a position to evaluate the fluctuating social dynamics as they relate to the lives of the clients. A casual look or visit to a community does not usually reveal many of the public and social service needs of that community. Transportation could be a major problem for families who do not own an automobile. The trash and garbage might not be picked up adequately. There might be insufficient play and recreational areas. Childcare services could be lacking. Inadequate drains and sewers could pose unsanitary conditions. Dilapidated housing, clutter of debris, unclean streets and grounds and junked automobiles could be factors that undermine community pride. The community might have a high incidence of crime, delinquency, school dropouts, unemployment and disease. An on the scene, eye witness worker, can better help the clients find their way through their maze of problems. Many of these problems and their effects on human behavior can be recognized only by a professionally trained worker who is based in the community.

The following excerpt by R.M. Carter provides a strong justification for community-based social service programs:

> The offender's predicament stems from the combination of personal deficits and social malfunctions that produced a criminal event and a social status. Most personal deficits characterizing offenders are also commonly

found in nonoffenders. The social malfunctions of unemployment, discrimination, economic inequity, and congested urban living affect most citizens. The offender, like other citizens, must find a way to live with his deficits and with the disorder around him. If corrections are to mitigate alienation, it must mobilize the community services that can make such an outcome possible.

The concept of community outreach social service delivery as advocated in this work must not be confused with the so-called, "do-gooder" approach of helping people out of a self-exalting condescending attitude. This approach involves helping people to understand their problems and helping them to help themselves based on a shared common community perspective. If this is to be a shared perspective the client and worker must be able to identify with each other. The primary helping ingredient is found in the sympathetic social and interpersonal relationship between the client and the worker. The helping relationship can be developed more completely by community outreach centers in the client's neighborhood.

The greatest potential for helping clients with social service needs is the active involvement of the client in his own helping process toward becoming independent and self-sustaining. This process involves not only overcoming personal problems but environmental ones as well. Working with the client without an intimate knowledge of his environment is analogous to trying to drive an automobile in the jungle or trying to grow a rose in the desert. Both can be done, but environmental modifications must be considered. A football player must be taught to play on the field, a boxer in the ring. It is difficult, if not impossible, to teach a person to swim away from water. The outreach worker can be more effective because he provides his expertise on the turf of the client, where the action is.

The educational resourcefulness of a professional worker in the community setting could result in significant benefits to the residents as well as to the municipality in which they live. Most professionals work in very structured situations where only specialized knowledge is disseminated, such as in a classroom, a particular job in a hospital, court or some other agency. And the clientele they cater to must have a narrow-specialized interest. However, many of the community residents have a multitude of diverse needs. An outreach worker who is a professional generalist in the areas of social services would be most helpful in attempting to satisfy these diverse needs. Unlike the specialized subjects taught in the school systems for long-range goals, general relevant information for many community dwellers is needed for immediate day-by-day survival.

The role of the outreach professional is designed to be just the opposite of that of the police. The police officer is a mobile-type community worker. Because of his uniform, security equipment and marked motor vehicle, the police officer has high visibility. He is also an authoritarian figure. The nature of his law enforcement job is inherently threatening. Such a threatening role serves as a barrier to a close helping relationship. For that reason, the outreach professional must be nonthreatening, and nonauthoritarian with low community visibility.

Many citizens forego social services because they cannot afford the expense or cope with the difficulties involved in their attainment. There is frequently a wide gap between the availability and accessibility of goods and services for persons of limited education, low income and other disadvantages associated with poverty. Unemployment benefits, food stamps, surplus food, family counseling, youth services, drug treatment, vocational rehabilitation, workmen's compensation, educational assistance and countless other social service programs are available. However, because of their urban centralization and bureaucratic administration, it is often a monumental task for the average poor person to gain access to available goods and services.

As the urban areas become more congested and as the bureaucracies get bigger, there is a continuing need for the decentralization of social and public service agencies at the community level. A community-based outreach program with a staff of professional outreach workers could substantially facilitate and increase the consumption of available goods and services. Their community location can serve to reduce the red tape and time period for social service delivery.

A particular centralized social service agency located downtown or in some other places in the city or county might have an abundant supply of goods and services. However, if these goods and services are inaccessible to the people in need, their consumption is not possible. The function of the outreach worker is not to provide all of the services but to be a referral source to assist in their procurement.

R. M. Carter makes the following analysis concerning community-based treatment:

... If behavior is related to events and circumstances in the offender's milieu, changing his behavior in isolation from that would not solve the problem. Evidence of behavioral change in the isolation of the total institution is meaningless. It is behavior at home, on the job, and on the streets that matters.

A basic principle underlying the philosophy of community-based corrections is that all efforts consistent with the safety of others should be made to reduce the involvement of the individual offender with the institutional aspects of corrections.

In most instances, the above analysis would apply to social services to the disadvantaged outside the correctional or criminal justice areas. There is a certain stigma and dependency-fostering aspect to many welfare programs.

The idea of community-based outreach services with outreach workers has implications for most, if not all of the bureaucratic centralized public and social service agencies. It offers a challenge to these agencies to decentralize their services and remove the gap between availability and accessibility.

CHAPTER 7
A GUIDE FOR PLANNING THE COMMUNITY PROGRAM

Alvin W. Cohn, Vice-President, Criminal Justice Associates, Rockville, Md. and Principal Associate of Planning Research Corporation in McLean, Virginia, attributes the failure of correctional institutions, to inadequate and incompetent management and leadership by correctional executives." He states that correctional managers have no professional body of knowledge upon which to base procedures and that they usually resort to rules and manuals. Cohn suggests that it is the manager of many of the correctional programs who cause such programs to fail. He states that "those managers who are willing to take risks and innovate programs for the benefit of their clients know that they frequently stand alone and are subject to the severe judgments of the powers that be, who are least qualified to evaluate the substantive aspects of their programs." Cohn suggests that correctional officials ought to demand money for basic and applied research to develop guidelines for evaluating programs instead of money to hire more personnel and build bigger and better facilities. He expresses the opinion that adequate management would provide society with relevant and significant organizational services.

A study of the correctional "nonsystem" in California by Robert E. Keldgord and others (Quotations of the word nonsystem is used by Keldgord) revealed the following: (1) no agreement as to goals, (2) minimal use of classification, (3) inadequate program and treatment, (4) poor intergovernmental relations, (5) insufficient public education, (6) outmoded organizational structure, (7) deficient correctional facilities. (8) lack of training, and (9) inappropriate allocation of funds.

The significant increase in community-based programs in the past few years suggests a lot of change and uncertainty concerning the future of these programs. Competent planning can increase their effectiveness. "Planning is the means by which the impact of uncertainty and change is diminished. Although planning does not overcome uncertainty and change completely, planning undertaken on a rational, systematic basis tends to take the "surprise" element out of future conditions of change."

"Internally, the planner is concerned with perfecting the tools of management, of being able on the one hand to keep the broad perspective with which he is charged and yet at the same time to fulfill individual assignments in relation to one another and to the big picture."

The specific objective of the community program must be spelled out clearly. The need for the community program and the expected accomplishments of such a program should be established. It is important to spell out the objectives of the program because every phase of its structure must be geared toward the accomplishment of the objectives. The objectives, goals and expected accomplishments will become the primary selling points of the program. The benefits and how the benefits are to be derived should be specified in the objective enumeration. The equipment used and the personnel assigned and their job descriptions will be in accord with the objectives of the program.

After the objectives have been clearly stated, a methodology for the accomplishment of these objectives must be formulated. One of the first considerations is the scope of the community program. The following questions must be answered: What kind of services will be provided? How many communities and clients do you plan to serve and over what time period? What are the guidelines and qualifications for the clients' eligibility and participation in the program? A specific client selection process must be defined to avoid any confusion as to who qualifies for the program. A criterion with the use of quantifiable data should be designed to measure the effectiveness of the program.

Based on the scope of the planned community program, the number and type of personnel to carry out the program must be determined. What kind of professionals are needed to do the work? What are the qualifications? Frequently, the sponsoring agency or its merit system will already have some of the professional positions and qualifications classified.

When the number and classification of employees have been determined, it is important to go a step further and clarify their employment status. Are the positions permanent or temporary? Do the community workers have a parallel employment status with their agency counterparts if there is such a sponsoring agency? Are the salaries and fringe benefits of the community workers the same as those of the regular staff at the main office?

It is important that the employment status, salaries and fringe benefits be equitable between the employees on the regular staff and in the community programs. Otherwise, serious morale problems will develop. When a group of employees with the same agency have the same job classifications and qualifications as other members of the staff and receive a lower salary and fewer job benefits, the differential treatment is detrimental to the special community program.

When it is necessary for a community program to be of a temporary nature because of the funding source or other factors, special consideration must be given to the employees who go into the community program. They must be given an equal opportunity for permanent job status where there is a Civil Service system. If no permanent positions are available, the community workers should be paid at a higher rate than are their permanent or regular counterparts to compensate for the risk of unemployment when the program is terminated. Additional compensation should be paid to the community worker because of the higher exposure to personal danger in a community setting. It is apparent that there is more personal security at the centralized office building. The central office building usually has a high concentration of people and is usually located among other commercial buildings.

The future employment status of the community workers should be given every consideration. If the community program proves worthy, every effort should be made to institutionalize it. These matters should be settled with as much finality as possible before implementing the Program.

Edward S. Greenberg's study of American workers reveals that they are generally unhappy. He says, " ... that unhappiness expresses itself through a wide range and variety of disorders: excessive drinking and drug use, psychosomatic illness, alienation, violence, despair and resignation."

Much of the unhappiness of workers expresses itself in administrative appeals and lawsuits. In its just ended 1975-76 term, the U.S. Supreme Court has decided more public employment cases than in any other term within memory. According to F. Arnold McDermott merit systems are under fire because of several significant influences and threats which confront them. He says, "the most important of these are: management discontent with merit systems; the patronage of sophistication; the rise of federal paternalism; and the power of collective bargaining." Poor planning, incompetent management and inequitable employment practices contribute to program failure and employee alienation.

The personnel organization chart must be drawn to show the relative position of each employee in the community program. If there is a sponsoring agency or regular staff, its personnel organizational chart should be illustrated in relation to the community program's personnel organization chart. No employee in the program should be directly responsible to more than one supervisor.

The personnel organization chart must show how each employee fits and functions in the program and the supervising accountability hierarchy.

A detailed job description must be prepared for each employee. This is necessary because of the few precedents set for community based professional social services. The job description helps the employee to focus his or her attention on the community aspect of his job at an early stage of his orientation. The community aspect of the job makes a significant difference. For example, the jobs of Social Worker, Counselor, Probation Officer, Teacher, etc. are not unusual or unique. However, when these services are provided in a community setting, a unique aspect might be added to these traditional social service jobs. The innovation of the community outreach program is not necessarily found in the service provided, but rather. where it is provided in the social dynamic setting of a community. An accurate and helpful job description must include an emphasis on job performance in the community setting.

Employees to work in the program can be recruited from an already hired regular staff or from a current register of new employees or a mixture of both. The advantage of selecting regular employees is that they have acquired institutional experience in their jobs. They are familiar with the work guidelines, policies, rules and regulations of the agency. Many of the regulars would have some familiarity with the community. Most of the social service workers on the regular staff would need only specific training and orientation in providing community-based services.

The primary disadvantage of using regular staff workers in a community program is their frequent tendency to return to the centralized office out of habit and personal attachment to other former co-workers. Such adherence to the central office and former staff associates could be distracting and disruptive to the community programs. Many regular workers who are transferred into the community program do not achieve the same sense of personal security in the community-based office as they experienced in the central office. It is not uncommon for members of the regular staff, as well as some new recruits, to reject employment in the community because of security reasons.

New employees who are hired specifically for the community program, not having been stationed at the central office, will usually adjust more readily to the new situation in the community. However, the new employees require a longer period of training than those recruited from the regular staff. The training needs and a time frame to meet those needs must be planned for the new and regular employees. A mixture of half new and half regular employees would facilitate and shorten the training process. Whatever selection process is used, it must not interfere with equal employment opportunities for any staff members.

Sufficient equipment and supplies must be ordered to accommodate the program and the personnel. Consideration must be given to office equipment such as desks, chairs, tables, bookcases, typewriters, and other necessary equipment and supplies to operate the program.

Each worker must have an individual workstation with all necessary equipment and supplies. There must be no conflict or competition regarding space in the offices. Adequate designated office space for each employee enhances a feeling of belonging and security for each worker as well as improving job performance.

In addition to the regular office equipment and supplies, adequate utilities and telephone service are essential. The community office must be clean, comfortable, and well maintained with janitorial services and basic toiletries. The social service workers' effectiveness will be minimized if they have janitorial responsibilities. This should not be a part of their job description. However, an employee in the program could be hired specifically for building maintenance and custodial care of the outreach offices if such services are not otherwise provided.

A client selection process must be developed to screen the defined clientele population to be served. The eligibility requirements must be defined so that there will be no question as to who qualifies for the program. Depending on the nature of the program, there might be such requirements as age, education, income, physical or mental handicaps, residential location, police record, school record or other such criteria. The eligibility criteria can be used to do research or conduct surveys in the community to identify the size and availability of the client population to be served.

After the client selection process has been defined, a method must be developed to get the actual prospective participants into the program. The participation may be voluntary or involuntary depending on the nature of the referrals or status of the clients. Some agencies, such as criminal justice, schools, public welfare and others having certain jurisdiction over clients, can require their participation in many cases. If the program depends on volunteer participants, some type of persuasion or other inducement must be used. The availability of clients is crucial to the operation of the program. Therefore, the availability of clients and their participation must be assured before the program is approved for funding or implementation.

An itemized detailed budget reflecting the total cost of the program must be developed. The budget must be drawn to cover a certain period of time to show the total cost for one year or two years or for whatever time period of operation is planned.

The budget should allow for salary increases, fringe benefits and increased costs of equipment and operation. In addition to the detailed budget, a budget narrative should be written to further explain and justify the total cost of the program. Some projections on cost-benefit analysis can be included. The detailed budget should also reflect the percentage of federal grant money and all other contributions to the program.

When the program is completely planned and has received all necessary approvals for implementation, a brief brochure explaining what the program is about should be developed for distribution. An attractive easy to read brochure with a graphic symbol and title relating to the program will encourage interest in the program. The distribution of the brochure will inform not only the staff but other inquirers from the outside as well. The brochure handout will also save the staff members time, by avoiding the constant repetition of explaining the program to the numerous interested persons and groups. It can serve as an aid in winning acceptance by the sponsoring agency and staff.

The information brochure can be used to enhance good public relations concerning the program. It is an indispensable aid in selling the idea of the community-based program to the management and residents of the community where the program is to be established.

Chapter 8
COMMUNITY OUTREACH OFFICE ACCOMMODATIONS

There are some options for office accommodations in the communities. The type of services provided, number of clients served, and the objectives of the program will be determining factors in selecting office accommodations. However, there are three categories of office accommodations to be considered when selecting community-based services. They are:

1. The modular unit or mobile home type structure.
2. The leased building or leased apartment type.
3. The leased space within an office or community agency building.

The modular unit or mobile home-type structure can be purchased and situated in an approved location by the management of the community. These structures are usually not desirable for community outreach services because they are conspicuous and isolated and therefore easy targets for theft and vandalism. Such high visibility could interfere with the assimilation of the staff with the community residents. The high visibility can more easily be interpreted as a threat or an outside intrusion. These kinds of general interpretations could detract from the operation of the community center. Since the outreach program will be serving a selected group of clients, constant high visibility to the community is probably more of a detriment. However, this might not be applicable in all instances.

Modular units can be an inconvenience in relocating to other communities. A new site must be found suitable for its location and negotiations must be arranged. This might not be an easy task because residents frequently reject the location of such structures in their communities. Also, upon relocating the modular unit, all utilities must be terminated and transferred to the new location. When and if the program is terminated, some efficient means of disposing of the unit must be considered.

A leased building or an apartment in the community can be used for the outreach office. Such a building or apartment would have a low visibility because it blends with other community structures. However, as in the modular unit, the outreach agency would have to be responsible for the utilities, janitorial services and security.

The modular unit, leased building and leased apartment are particularly vulnerable to theft and vandalism when the offices are closed at night, on weekends and on holidays. The outreach staff is considered as tenants of these units and they are directly responsible for their security.

The third category is the leased space within an office or community agency building. These buildings are the traditional types that are generally accepted in the communities. The types of buildings referred to are schools, churches, health centers, YMCA, Boys' Clubs, parks and recreation and other multiple purpose neighborhood buildings. Most communities, especially those with apartment complexes, have management offices. These offices frequently have space for community service accommodation. This third category of leased space within an already established community building appears to be the most advantageous for community-based services. The owners or proprietors of these buildings usually have their own security personnel for the entire building. They usually have central utilities and janitorial services. In addition to these conveniences, reception service is frequently provided. The building with another or several other social service agencies is helpful in having additional resources in the same building and coordination of services with the staff of the other agencies.

There are some other important advantages and fringe benefits in acquiring leased space within an already established community building or multiple purpose center. Many of the larger buildings have cafeterias, snack bars, conference rooms, water fountains, libraries, etc. Many of the agencies within the building form coordination councils and sponsor other joint activities.

Many resources are often developed and shared by various agencies. Some of the agencies distribute periodic newsletters and post other announcements of current interests. This teamwork approach is often of mutual benefit to all of the agencies. It enhances the morale of the staff and prevents the isolation of staff members. An isolated staff can pose certain hazards in personal relationships for members of the community staff as well as for the clients. This is especially true in male-female encounters. Women in many instances are fearful of being left alone in a community office that accommodates the public. A locked office cannot fully carry out the intended function of the outreach program. The safety factor must be taken into consideration. The buildings which house multiple agencies solve most of the problems mentioned above. There is presently a healthy trend on the part of many state and local agencies toward the establishment of multiple-purpose centers in many communities.

Community changes and population shifts might necessitate relocating an outreach office. Relocating outreach offices is made simpler by lease agreements. It usually involves a minimum of thirty days' notice to terminate a lease agreement. A new location and new lease agreement can often be accomplished in a short period.

The procedure for acquiring community outreach offices is usually done through the management office and representatives of the community residents. Many communities have tenant or resident associations or a comparable group by some other name. These are usually formal organizations with regularly scheduled meetings.

One of the best approaches to acquiring community accommodations is to set appointments with the community leaders, representatives and management and explain the program to them and ask for their support. They must first be sold on the idea. It is important to approach both residents and management.

Usually, after approval has been received from the management and residents, a lease agreement is drafted. It is advantageous for the Director of the outreach program to be involved in the negotiation of the agreement in order to know all of the conditions of the lease. The actual drafting of the lease agreements may be done by the legal department of the outreach or rental agency.

The acquisition of community accommodations for an outreach program involves much more than the leasing of a building or apartment or the setting up of a modular unit. It involves selling the idea of the program to the community and its representatives. It involves winning community acceptance for the location of the community-based program in the respective community. If this is not done the program might not get the necessary support and cooperation for its success or continuation.

CHAPTER 9
SOME PERSONNEL TRAINING ESSENTIALS

The training essentials will be determined primarily by the objectives of the Community Program and the nature and policy of the sponsoring agency. In addition to the sponsor's training requirements, it is recommended that each employee be trained in his specific job description before he is placed in the community and before he starts receiving assignments in the community. There are exceptions when the employee is under close competent supervision.

The probability for error and mismanagement is higher and more costly in the more unstructured community setting than the more structured centralized office. Mistakes and blunders on the part of untrained staff members can cause irreparable damage to the outreach project's image in the community.

A high degree of resourcefulness is required of the outreach worker because he is not surrounded by office personnel with an immediate supply of answers to the many questions that will arise in the community. In order that he might be expeditious in his decisions and actions, the outreach worker must be trained and knowledgeable about the policies and procedures of the agency he represents. His effectiveness as a community worker will depend upon his knowledge, experience and resourcefulness as a representative of his or her agency. Deficiencies in these areas could even cause serious misrepresentations of the sponsoring agency.

A liberal arts education provides a foundation which is most helpful for social service workers. A general knowledge of sociology, psychology, the other social sciences and the humanities is expected to be a part of their training. However, along with this foundation, it is expected that the social service worker will have substantial experience in working with people and also a high degree of social and emotional maturity.

In addition to the general background of training described above, some training in the following areas is considered essential for community based outreach workers:

1. General community orientation with an emphasis on the people and the social service resources.
2. Facilitation skills in counseling for individuals, families, groups, crisis intervention and group therapy.
3. Supportive casework services.
4. Concepts of Behavior Modifications, Reality Therapy and Transactional Analysis.
5. Community organization with respect to institutions of religion, educational institutions, politics and law.
6. Communication skills, public speaking, public relations and affirmative action.

The training essentials mentioned above are not meant to be an exhaustive list. They serve as a general guideline for training social service workers to be able to function at the highest level of preparedness in a community setting. They do not guarantee success. They are aids in carrying out the science and art of social service work.

In many instances, the recruits for the particular jobs have had certain valuable experiences that would be beneficial to the group if shared. It can often be beneficial to explore the unique experiences, talents and skills of the new employees. Frequently, the sharing of abilities among staff members can bring about more cohesion and teamwork. A person's background and social class can also be factors that enhance or detract from his job performance. Numerous studies done in various parts of the country have consistently concluded that the social class level of the family is related to the level of occupational aspiration.

CHAPTER 10
THE OPERATION OF COMMUNITY OUTREACH CENTERS

In as much as accessibility is the key consideration in outreach services, the centers must be located in the communities where the services are to be provided. The lower-status socio-economic communities are usually the ones most in need of outreach social services. The outreach centers must be located among the population to be served to maximize the benefits. They serve primarily as a base of operation for the outreach workers. It is not the purpose of the center to be a substitute for traditional agencies, such as schools, EOA Centers, churches, community clubs, hospitals, courts, Goodwill Industries, etc.

The primary purpose is to get the clients involved with the appropriate agencies that provide the needed services. Many clients are not aware of the resources in their own communities. One of the outreach objectives is to assist the client, first of all, in the utilization of community resources. The outreach program, among other things, is a bridge that leads to help, preferably, self-help.

A large community might require further decentralization of the outreach centers into surrounding satellite offices. This will depend on the size, population density and number of neighborhoods to be served and, of course, the availability of the outreach staff.

The concentration of more than four staff members at one center should be avoided. However, the number of staff will necessarily vary with the quantity, quality, and intensity of services to be provided. Using a minimum number of staff members at each center helps to avoid recentralization of services. Where there is sufficient staff the services can be expanded by the use of satellite offices.

A small office with a desk, a couple of chairs and a telephone is usually the major equipment required in a satellite office. In many instances the satellite accommodations can be gotten free or at a nominal fee.

Generally, an outreach center with ten social service workers could have four or five satellite offices with one or two workers in each. Therefore, a staff of twelve, a supervisor, secretary and ten outreach workers could establish five office locations in a section of the city or area to be served.

The supervisor and secretary would operate from the main outreach office. Such administrative functions as the assignment of cases, timekeeping, reporting, training, staff meetings and other personnel matters are to be conducted from the main outreach office. The supervision of outreach personnel is simplified by schedules, reporting systems and the direct communication by telephone with the satellite offices. In some instances it is feasible to install computer terminals in the outreach offices.

Specific assignment of areas or communities for each outreach worker enables the worker to concentrate his efforts and thereby intensify the impact of his services within defined geographical boundaries. The area assignment has the advantage of reducing the time and expense of traveling and crisscrossing the city or county to work with and serve clients within the service jurisdiction. The assigned areas afford more time to work intensively with the clients. It provides a greater opportunity for the worker to get acquainted with the people and resources in his or her assigned community. Broad services and areas usually minimize the quality and intensity of the services provided. The assigned areas and satellite offices help to maximize benefits and intensify services.

The assignment of personnel to the outreach offices must be done with careful consideration in order to avoid time-consuming personnel problems and to promote maximum efficiency in the operation of the community program. Because the director of the outreach project will seldom get directly involved with the clients, his or her location in the community outreach office is not mandatory. However, the supervisors should be located in the outreach offices in order to provide the leadership and the close and appropriate supervision necessary.

Another consideration is to avoid assigning outreach workers in such a manner as to get in each other's way or to have conflicting problems or assignments. Each worker must have individually assigned responsibility of his own with the necessary authority and freedom to carry out the assignment. Each worker must have the responsibility and accountability for his assigned duties. The duties must be delineated as clearly as possible.

When two or more workers are assigned the same duties, services are often needlessly duplicated and staff participation is unnecessarily limited and hampered. Both result in an inefficient allocation of resources. This type of inefficiency frequently results when two people work as partners, in teams or where there is a worker with an assistant.

Sometimes the attachments can become so inseparable that two workers are performing the job of one person. Both workers in this described partnership situation can unintentionally inhibit the work potential and professional growth of the other.

The teamwork and partnership working relationships can be damaging to the individual initiative and creativity of both workers unless carefully paired and properly supervised. The male-female work relationships are particularly vulnerable to the development of unproductive types of vocational propinquity in community based services. The male worker has a tendency to be overly protective, overly accommodating and in some instances, overly aggressive with his female co-worker. However, many of these partnerships or teamwork relationships work out very well. There are many variables to be considered.

The success of a community outreach program will depend to a great extent on the degree of involvement with the community organizations. Many of the community concerns are expressed at community meetings where there is grassroots participation. The high level professional meetings concerning community plans and needs are helpful in understanding the communities. The news media coverage aids in understanding the general problems of certain communities. However, the occasional high level planners' meetings by representatives of the appropriate governmental agencies and the news coverage from a distance concerning community affairs do not capture the intimate concerns and social atmosphere of the residents of the community. These intimate concerns can only be learned by grassroots participation and involvement.

One of the most effective ways of getting involved with the community residents is to attend their meetings and participate in their organizations. Many communities have residential associations, coordinating councils, Parent

Teacher Student Associations, and religious, civic, social, and other citizen neighborhood groups.

Many of these groups have regular meetings and invite participants to serve on projects and committees. These offer an inroad to involvement for the community outreach workers. These meetings provide learning experiences and an opportunity to inform the community about the Community Outreach Program. They also provide an opportunity for good public relations services.

The three general social service categories for an outreach program are remedial, preventive, and promotional. The remedial programs are geared toward rehabilitative services. These categories may be in many areas, such as crime, delinquency, school dropouts, truancy, unemployment, physical and mental handicaps, drug and alcohol treatment, etc. The remedial areas are those where the damage has already been done.

The preventive category is designed to prevent the occurrence of problems that would require remediation. Successful preventive programs have the potential to alleviate the need for remedial programs. Preventive programs are usually less expensive. However, one of the difficulties with preventive programs is to identify potential clients or problems. Clients for remedial programs are more obvious and consequently easier to identify than the potential ones for a preventive type program.

Because there are great needs for remedial and preventive type special programs, promotional type programs are not as common. Promotional programs are designed to assist clients who are not classified as delinquents or failures or handicapped or who suffer other special deficits. Promotional programs are designed to assist clients to excel or participate in some area of development or competency not usually related to handicapping deprivation. Successful clients and clients with special abilities may also qualify to participate in a promotional type of program. Promotional services are characterized by elevative and accelerative efforts and activities.

There is not always a hard line of division among the three general categories of social services. There are preventive aspects to many remedial programs and vice versa. There are preventive aspects to many promotional programs and the reverse is also true in this case. These service categories can also be integrated into a single program. An example of an integrated social service program that includes the remedial, preventive and promotional aspects is a student tutorial program whereby advanced students are paid to tutor retarded and less advanced students. The three general service categories help define and distinguish the service areas for various reasons.

A community outreach program must develop some form of screening and intake process. Usually, there will be walk-in type clients or referred clients who do not officially qualify for the program.

A short term counseling or referral process should be set up for the unofficial clients. This will avoid the impression that people are turned away without any services. People seeking help with urgent needs have low tolerance levels for lectures on guidelines that are not relevant to their needs. In a community setting it is especially important that all clients be treated with courtesy. Failure to do so could result in unfavorable public relations in the community or worse. The main or central outreach office should be the office equipped to handle intake and record keeping.

It is sound policy for the outreach workers to identify with the residents on a high level of social responsibility.

Experience has taught that well-groomed and appropriately attired community workers have a better professional working image among the residents than those workers who practice the more unconventional ways of dressing, which are commonly associated with "fad" fashions. It is important that the worker's appearance, as well as his conduct, be a positive influence.

The operation of the community-based offices must be carried out with the highest professional and ethical standards. They must be places where sound business and administrative practices are adhered to. They must not be places where unethical, illegal, or immoral conduct takes place. Such conduct will destroy the credibility of the program and cause the residents and clients to lose respect for the community project. They must not be places to loiter or hang out. The general atmosphere of a community-based office should be one of positive and constructive activities. Its operation should be an example worthy of emulation and a credit to everyone involved.

The residents must be convinced by the sound operation of the outreach centers and the conduct of the workers that they are in the community for business as helping professionals and not for social experimentation.

Policies must be formulated to achieve this goal. The problems of policy in business, like those of policy in public affairs, have to do with the choice of purposes, the molding of organizational character, the definition of what needs to be done, and the mobilization of resources for the attainment of goals in the face of competition or adverse circumstances."

According to Harold Koontz and Cyril O'Donnell, the function of a manager is the proper utilization of the process of planning, organizing, staffing, directing and controlling. These processes are the logical framework within which to classify the basic practice and knowledge of management. In addition to these functions, it is also the manager's job to formulate policies and develop corporate strategies to accomplish the objectives and goals of the organization.

CHAPTER 11
MANAGEMENT AND STRUCTURE OF THE PROGRAM

The general theory of management of this thesis is based primarily on the ideas of Claude S. George.' According to George, managers create an environment conducive to the performance of acts by other individuals (1) to accomplish a collective objective or goal, commonly called the firm's goal, and (2) to achieve one or more of the goals of the participating individuals. Determining the collective objectives of an undertaking and generating an environment for their achievement is the total function of a manager according to George.

He states that the environment which managers create can be described as being of two types. One is physical and the other is conceptual. The physical climate consists of the fixtures, the materials, the tools, the methods and sequencing. In its conceptual aspects, the environment generated by managers has to do with the individual minds of the workers. It is not a collective mind according to George, but is aimed at creating a frame of mind in each worker that will enable him to understand why it is to his advantage to expand his efforts to achieve the total or firm objective, it being "to his advantage" only when it enables him directly or indirectly to reach his personal goal or goals.

The general management theory of Claude S. George, as well as many other social service management theorists studied, has relevant application to the successful management of a community based social service program. Its application in the preparation of this thesis has been attempted.

All parts of the community program must be brought together in a definite functional unit. Fragmentations must be eliminated and the loose ends pulled together. Every staff member must understand his role and expected job performance within the organizational structure. It is important for a manager to understand thoroughly how to delegate responsibility and authority.

The success of an outreach program will depend greatly on the teamwork of the staff. Teamwork involves a delicate balance between individual and group efforts. Each member of the community team must know and perform his job well. Each must know the goals of the project so that his efforts will be geared toward the accomplishment of those goals. Each person should be encouraged to develop his skills and proficiency in his job to the maximum feasible extent.

In order to effect a meaningful structure in the lives and habit patterns of others, the outreach staff must effect such a structure for its own organization and operation. Consistent and systematic procedures and schedules must be developed for the performance of duties. Records must be kept accurate, complete and current at all times.

Frequent and free flowing communication among the staff is important. Communication can be done in staff meetings, by telephone, memoranda, letters, person to person-,, individually and in groups. These various methods should be used in consideration of priorities, urgency and the nature of the business at hand.

Communication with other staff members must be done so as to minimize the distraction from their work, the interference of their schedules and the consumption of valuable time. The more staff members engage each other in unplanned and unscheduled conversations, meetings and encounters the less time there is to perform the job. Therefore, each staff member must be encouraged to schedule his time and respect the scheduled time of other staff members. There is a danger of a community-based program losing its outreach thrust to excessive internal preoccupation.

The outreach centers and workers must have an operational schedule reflecting the following information:

1. Name of center and telephone number.
2. Supervisor's name.
3. Address of center.
4. Days and hours of operation during the week.
5. The name and position title of all personnel assigned to the center or satellite offices, work schedules, address and telephone numbers.
6. A general description of the services provided, when and where they are provided.

There is room for flexibility in the schedules geared to meet social service needs. However, there must be a dependable consistency. To a great extent, the clientele must revolve around the outreach workers' schedules. The schedules must be set practically to deal with most of the clients' problems most of the time. That which is lost by the limits of flexibility will be gained by the reliability of consistency. The operating schedules will minimize confusion for the staff as well as for the clients.

A schedule geared to meet almost everyone's needs most any time usually does not meet anyone's needs adequately at any special time. There will be those exceptional circumstances that require out of schedule handling. However, one must avoid letting the exceptional cases disrupt his schedule to the point of not having a schedule. The fact that there are many circumstances and needs which do not fit into a schedule, is really an argument for a schedule.

People generally appreciate organizational structure and consistency. The assurance that a service will be available at consistent times is more reliable and accessible than a service at inconsistent times. A consistent schedule enables the worker as well as the clients and others to plan and therefore, minimize the interference with other obligations and responsibilities. The objective of organizational structure and operation is to maximize the delivery of social services from a community-based outreach program.

CHAPTER 12
SUMMARY AND CONCLUSIONS

The primary purpose of this thesis is to provide general guidelines for the establishment and operation of a community-based outreach program based on an inside view of its internal operations. This is a general analysis of the concept, organizational structure and operational functions of a community program. This is not intended to be a model for a specific program, such as a juvenile delinquency or other crime prevention program. It is intended to be a general model for various kinds of social service programs.

This model is designed to be general enough to include helpful guidelines for various types of community programs and sufficiently specific to embrace the basic philosophy of all such programs. There is a wide variety of social service programs that could increase the accessibility of their services by community decentralization.

A review of the literature reveals that there is a lack of published material on how to set up and operate a community based social service program. There is a lack of attention given to the quality of personnel who work in these programs. There is a lack of information on the impact the community program has on the sponsoring agency, the community and the people who work in the program. The literature reflects a lack of consideration and appreciation for the multiple human elements that constitute a community program.

The heart of a community is its people. The heart of a community program is the people who work in the program.

Therefore, any comprehensive studies or analyses on community programs must take into consideration the intimate and sensitive "flesh and blood" issues of the people and those things that impact on their lives. This includes the working conditions, employment opportunities, the adequacy and quality of equipment and supplies, the quality of the social relationships, the managerial efficiency and the nobility of purpose of the program.

Community based programs demand radically new roles for the clients, workers and citizens. They place new responsibilities on the sponsoring agencies to accommodate the changes and innovations of the new program. They challenge the sponsoring agency to provide equal employment opportunities for its employees who are more vulnerable to the hazards of alienation from their agency counterparts and the high exposure to a more unstructured community and environment.

The potential benefits of community programs have barely been tapped. It is hoped that this model will provide a framework that will lend insight and aid in realizing the greatest social service potential of community-based outreach programs.

PART THREE

FOUNDATIONS FOR YOUTH TRANSFORMATION

CHAPTER 13
IMPACT OF AMERICAN SHIFTING VALUES

Core Values of America

These core values served America well. They have made America the most prosperous and the most powerful country on earth. These values have afforded the citizens and inhabitants of America more freedom and opportunities than any other country on earth. These values must be asserted by all people of goodwill who value freedom and God's gift of human life:

1. One Nation under God.
2. Judeo-Christian Holy Bible.
3. The Declaration of Independence.
4. Representative government by the people, for the people and of the people.
5. The Church of Christ.
6. The common language of English.
7. The Apostles' Creed.
8. The United States Constitution.
9. U.S. Motto-"In God We Trust."
10. The Pledge of Allegiance.
11. Individual Freedom.
12. Freedom of speech, religion, press, assembly.
13. Due process of law for life, liberty and property.
14. The equal protection of the law.
15. Self defense.

16. Freedom from unreasonable searches and seizures.
17. Respect for the dignity and sacredness of human life.
18. Freedom from involuntary servitude.
19. The institution of family and marriage between a man and a woman.
20. Compulsory school attendance for children.
21. Equal education and equal employment opportunities.
22. The free enterprise system.
23. Separation of governmental powers-Executive, Legislative and Judicial.
24. Redress of grievances.

This is not intended to be an exhaustive list of core American values. However, it is important for every American to be knowledgeable of their core values to appreciate the historical sacrifices and the importance of their perpetuation for generations to come. (Christian Institute of Public Theology) May 25, 2010.

The Core Problems of the American Society (Based on a public theological perspective)

1. The silence (or silenced) Enlightened Prophetic Voices.
2. The Retreat of the Church from the Public Life of Society and from the Raging Ideological Spiritual Warfare.
3. The Growing Compromise of Judeo-Christian Values with Idolatry and Secularism.
4. Spiritual Blindness and Rebellion Against the Revelatory

1. Knowledge and Light of God.
5. The Moral Relativity of Giving Credence to Arbitrary Opinions and Behaviors without Validated Truth or Merit.
6. Ethical Neutrality-The Failure to Give Witness to Truth or to Take a Righteous Stand or to Adhere to a Position of Equity and Justice.
7. The Loss of National Vision, Purpose and Direction along with the Corrosion of Governmental Privatization.
8. Indulgence of Self-Centered Individualism at the Expense of Diluting the Values Essential for the Common Good.
9. Cultural Confusion and Political Instability Influenced by Arbitrary and Capricious Decisions to find Favor with partisan Individuals and Groups of Diverse Ideological Backgrounds and Persuasions.
10. Educational Fragmentation with a Lack of a Unifying Comprehensive Purpose Driven Corporate Focus for the Common Good.
11. Diminishing Merit Systems That Have No Consistency and No Uniformity in Rewarding and Reinforcing Achievement and Success.
12. Lack of Equitable, Sound and Appropriately Elevated Standards as Measures and Incentives for the Growth, Progress and Security for the Common Good.

Most thoughtful men and women would agree with the enumerations of the above Core Problems. Many thoughtful and concerned men and women would also agree that there is an urgent need for A GREAT AWAKENING, A

RENAISSANCE, A MASSIVE REFORMATION, AND A TRANSCENDENT TRANSFORMATION.

Rev. Willie J. Webb, Author

The Way Out of Darkness: Vital Public Theology Actions to Turn the Lethal Tide

Human Effects of Demoralization

In the absence of strong positive visionary leadership, social organizations become unglued and fall apart. Thus, a permissive culture is created where everyone does what is right in his or her own eyes. (Judges 21:25). Therefore, an environment is created where the common goal of the whole human enterprise disintegrates into misguided individual conflicting goals, confusion and chaos. A socially disintegrating society where the moral compass and the traditional survival values have been disrupted, many people become demoralized.

Demoralization

Demoralization is the diminished desire of the human spirit to live and succeed. It is the progressive diminution of the will to live. It is the acceptance of defeat by the human spirit. Demoralization represents cooperation with the demoralizing forces by the victims who are being demoralized.

Some Root Causes of Demoralization

Some of the root causes of demoralization are as follows: injustice, heartbreak, rejection, dehumanization, disappointment, helplessness, hopelessness, adverse discrimination, deprivations, intimidations, subjugation, involuntary servitude, alienation, isolation, internalized anger, rage and fears.

Some Effects of Demoralization

1. Loss of confidence in others and self.
2. Loss of the feeling of self-worth.
3. Loss of self-esteem.
4. Loss of dreams.
5. Loss of vision for the future.
6. Loss of future hope.
7. Loss of autonomy.
8. Loss of spirit to confront and challenge obstacles.
9. Loss of the spirit to care about life.
10. Loss of the spirit to fight for the values of life.
11. Loss of external and internal interests.
12. Loss of the spirit to live.

Some (Unhealthy) Methods Used in Coping with Demoralization

1. Denial of Reality— Self-deception.
2. Social avoidance-Self-imposed blindness and deafness to reality.
3. Rationalization- Create excuses and alibis to avoid facing reality.

4. Distortion-Create comfortable fantasies and delusions to avoid truth.
5. Projection-Select others or something else to place blame.
6. Psychological ventilation-Curse the darkness and fight the air.
7. Give up-Stop fighting and surrender to defeat.
8. Become irresponsible —Turn self over to other's care.
9. Sedation and tranquilization through alcohol and other drug addiction.
10. Become mentally and physically ill. Stop striving.
11. Criminality, theft, fraud, etc.-Wreak havoc on society.
12. Homicide, suicide and other forms of self-destruction.

Reversing Demoralization through Regeneration, Reformation and Transformation

The corrupted culture, misguided ideologies and permissive pathological environment can be ameliorated through competent God-connected, and God inspired leadership. There are scientific, rational and spiritual remedies for the list of root causes of our human demoralization. Demoralization is no mystery. The causes are known or knowable. Each root cause of demoralization can be isolated, studied, assessed and eliminated.

There are remedies and solutions for the debilitating effects of demoralization. There are answers and means to reverse the lethal tide of demoralization. The personnel, resources, methodologies and expertise exist to begin to get the job done. The individuals and institutions who clam to know the will, the ways, the wisdom and the works of God, must take the initiative to mobilize and utilize the personnel and resources to heal the land and restore the people of God. It is incumbent upon the enlightened clergy of God to develop the plans and strategies and provide theological guidance and leadership.

As long as we continue to evade the escalating crisis of our serious ethical, moral, spiritual and serious human predicament in America, the implosive, explosive and destructive demoralization will continue to take its lethal toll.

The Public Theologian
CAPT. Inc.
P.O. Box 3148
Atlanta. Georgia 30303-3148

Factors Associated with Juvenile Delinquency

Identifying the Potential Delinquent

SOME PREDICTIVE FACTORS

Home and Parental Influences

1. A child from a broken home.
2. A child from a low-income and low socio-economic status family.
3. A child with inadequate adult supervision due to poverty, apathy, alcoholism and ignorance.
4. A child who lives in an overcrowded home.
5. A child who feels rejected by his parents and unwanted at home.

6. A child from a home of confusion, turmoil and violence.
7. A child who is culturally deprived with an impoverished background.
8. A child, especially a boy, who lacks a father figure in the home.
9. A child from a problem home where there is sibling rivalry, jealousy and unstable parents.
10. A child with an abundance of unsupervised time.
11. A child with adverse influence from members of family or friends who are frequently in violation of the law, who serve as examples for the child.
12. A child from a home with little or no motivation from the parents and inconsistent disciplinary practices.
13. A child whose interests and goals for himself conflict with those of his parents for him.
14. A child from a home with poor parent child relationships.
15. A child from a home with conflicts involving child rejection, abuse and where child is used as a scapegoat by other members of the family.
16. A child from a family with a history of aggressive, hostile and erratic behavior in other family members.
17. A child who lacks spiritual training and comes from a home with an immoral climate.
18. A child who runs away from home and lives under conditions which precipitates such actions.
19. An unstable family situation; a child who is shuffled from one relative, friend or foster home to another.
20. A child who is caught in the undertow of poverty, family problems and peer group pressures.

Characteristics of Child

1. A child with low mental ability and improper parental guidance.
2. A child who lacks ambition and meaningful goals.
3. A child who lacks interest in hobbies, projects, other fun activities and who lacks involvement in school activities and productive work.
4. A child who is a loner with few friends or no friends.
1. Especially a child with poor peer group interaction.
5. A child who day dreams frequently to escape the world of reality.
6. A child who is unhappy, unfriendly, withdrawn and moody.
7. A child who is inclined toward dependency and fails to assume personal responsibility for their decisions and actions.
8. A child who fails to adjust socially during adolescence and turns to delinquency for acceptance and attention.
9. A child who disrespects resents and rebels against authority.
10. A child who lacks confidence and has a low self image.
11. A child who has basic character disorders: dishonesty, violent temper socio and psychopathic.
12. A child who is mentally and emotionally disturbed.
13. A child with poor sexual identity, development, control, adjustment and education.
14. A child who is angry and hostile toward others and exhibits misguided aggression.

15. A child who uses poor judgment in selecting peers for friends and associates. (Usually associates with peers who are failures and inclined toward delinquency.)
16. A child with drug or alcohol addiction or involvement.
17. A child with a history of repeated non-target type offenses and involvement.
18. A child who lacks respect for the rights, property and person of others.
19. A child who is impulsive, undisciplined and seeks immediate gratifications of his wants and desires.
20. A child who has insatiable desires and wants which exceed his tolerance level to wait, and his personal ability and economic means to satisfy.
21. A young male who is in the habit of carrying weapons, such as pistols, knives, etc. with the expectation and anticipation of trouble.
22. A child who is not constructively involved in the institutional programs provided by society and who consequently roams and loiters in areas which present him with many opportunities for delinquent activities.
23. A child who keeps late hours away from home and is a frequent curfew violator.
24. A child with a chip on his shoulder who seeks vengeance.
25. A child who seeks negative vindication.
26. A child who is inadequately equipped to travel the lawful road to legitimate success.
27. A child whose pathways to legitimate success have been blocked.

28. A child who feels a strong need to vindicate his status (prove his worth) as a human being, through negative and maladaptive behavior.

Influence of the School

1. A child who has dropped out of school.
2. A child who has a behavior problem and troublemaker at school.
3. A child who is an academic failure.
4. A child who is frequently truant from school.
5. A child who is frustrated and unhappy in school because of his inability to perform on grade level, thus having his self-image damaged by reinforcing his feelings of failure and inadequacy.

Characteristics and Influence of the Community

1. A child who lives in a blighted area with inadequate educational, cultural and recreational facilities in his community.
2. A child who lives in a community where there is a high rate of unemployment, welfare recipients, one parent families, idle young people with no constructive involvement and where crime and delinquency are common patterns of behavior.

SOME PRIMARY FAMILIAL AND PERSONAL DEFICIENCIES ASSOCIATED WITH JUVENILE DELINQUENTS

Home and Parental Deficiencies

1. A child who feels rejected, unwanted and unloved.
2. A child who lacks encouragement and motivation, often associated with poverty and family disorganization. There is often a lack of planning and future orientation with these type families.
3. A child with parents or guardians who lack basic skills essential to the adequate performance of the various social roles of parent, spouse, employee, domestic management, and participants in community affairs.
4. A child whose parents lack the necessary education, certification and marketable skills to acquire productive employment and consequently live in a perpetual state of uncertainty, insecurity and dependency.
5. A child with parents or a family member who are alcoholic or have poor emotional and mental health.
6. A child from a home where there is generally lack of nourishing food, appropriate clothing, educational resources, cultural exposure and religious training.
7. A child from an excessively crowded home situation with unsanitary living conditions, which does not afford sufficient comfort or minimum privacy essential for proper adjustment and development.
8. A child with disinterested parents who fail to give proper discipline and guidance and who often leave

the child alone to plan and make important decisions for himself.

9. A child who does not have what he considers a significant person or group to identify with. His absentee father has been defined as "no good." His frequently unavailable mother might be less than a "virtuous woman." He might not be a member of a church. His peer group might not allow him to belong.

10. A child with no "heroes" (highly esteemed persons) to admire and look up to, no guiding principals and no noble dreams to be realized.

11. A child whose parents have not found a proper balance between affection and discipline, rewards and punishment for the child.

12. A child deprived of a consistently stable home, especially the child who is trapped in the foster home cycle, having been shifted around for years.

13. A child who has not been taught, or one who has failed to learn, to respect the rights, the person and property of others.

14. A child who has been taught to distrust and disrespect people in general and authoritative persons in particular, e.g. adults, parents, teachers, police, etc.

15. A child who lacks moral and spiritual training and who has failed to internalize the socially acceptable values of the society.

16. A child who is emotionally deprived of acceptance, warmth, love and understanding especially by parents and peers.

17. A child caught up in the cross-fire of parental conflicts and who is used as a scapegoat for hostile adults to unload the wrath of their firey tongues. A child who

does not have any wholesome means of outlet or escape through sublimation or recreation.

18. A child from a family who lacks money or mismanages money to the extent of being financially unable to satisfy his personal needs and desires.

19. A child who sees himself as inferior and unattractive and feels that others consider him the same. A child who feels that others are o.k. and he is not o.k. and further, that he will not become o.k.

20. A child who is victimized or abused by a neurotic parent whose punishment for the child is based on projections of imaginary undesirable traits found in the parent and thought to exist in the child.

21. A child whose parent or guardian has had prolonged mental or physical illness, perhaps requiring hospitalization or a child whose parents are disabled, handicapped or deceased and adequate substitute parents have not been found.

22. A child who has given up because he feels that he lives in a hopeless situation. He might feel overwhelmed with personal and family inadequacy. The road of social mobility might seem too long and too steep for him to travel.

23. A child whose family fails to go the "second mile" in seeking vital help from social agencies for the welfare and future interest of the child.

Some Characteristics of Child Deficiencies

1. A child with poor development and poor health due to poor prenatal care and health care during early childhood.
2. A child who is extremely introverted with feelings of inadequacy and inability to compete.
3. A child with low mental ability, learning disabilities and difficulties.
4. A child who is unable to read or have any success ratio.
5. Improper sex education and attitude toward sex causing perversion or other maladjustments, such as homosexuality, promiscuity, etc.
6. A child who has failed to adjust socially during adolescence, thus causing him to turn to crime for attention or join delinquent "gangs" for acceptance.

School Related Deficiencies

1. A culturally disadvantaged child who fails to achieve academically and drops out of school.
2. A child whose ability and level of achievement do not permit him to adjust in the regular classroom and consequently get "turned off" by the school.
3. A child who is not placed in a learning situation commensurate with his abilities.
4. A child who is embarrassed at school because of his dress or dullness or some other factors which are threatening or destructive to his pride and self esteem.
5. A child who is shut out of those activities which are essential for a feeling of acceptance.

Some Characteristics of Community Deficiency

1. A child from a neighborhood of low socio-economic status which has a reputation for being bad; the child might see himself as part of his environment, and certain sub-cultural happenings are taken for granted. Such things as stealing, consuming alcohol, taking drugs, and being profane, loud and boisterous, maybe a way of life.

2. A child who lives in a community where there are inadequate recreational facilities and unsupervised group activities.

3. A child from a community that lacks adequate socializing agents- schools, churches, libraries, parks, museums, health clinics, clubs, etc.

4. A child from a community where there is social disorganization and moral deterioration, disunity and a lack of overall constructive purpose.

5. A child from a community where there is a concentration of social failure, poverty, high ratio of crime, high rates of divorce, separation, welfare recipients, mental illness, illegitimacy, etc.

GENERAL REMEDIAL AND SUPPORTIVE NEEDS
OF DELINQUENTS AND UNRULY CHILDREN

1. A concerned adult or supportive authoritative figure who will give some prime time and attention, and who will listen and understand.
2. A child needs supervision and guidance from at least two (male and female) mature adults, preferably the natural father and mother.
3. Every person and especially every child needs frequent high quality social relationships with at least one other person. A high-quality social relationship involves mutual friendship and trust. There is an absence of antagonism, threats, hostility, indifference, exploitation and negativism.
4. Children need to be able to relate to adults that they feel they can trust (with their feelings, thoughts and ideas) and who are genuinely interested in them; a person with whom they can discuss their problems.
5. Children need a good rapport with adults and good adult examples.
6. Children need to feel that someone has confidence in them, because they often live up to or down to what they consider our expectations of them.
7. A child needs an advocate, often, someone outside the family and outside the professional casework-client relationship who takes an active interest in the individual child; a VPO, "Big Brother," "Big Sister," a relative, volunteer or youth worker.
8. Children need to be able to identify with success types of their own ethnic and sex groups.

9. Children need strong but fair authority figures in their lives.
10. Children need well adjusted adults in the home, school and community, as models to relate to, identify with and to emulate.
11. Children need positive relationships with adults, authority figures, family and peers.
12. A child might need medical or some other type of professional treatment to overcome such problems as being overweight, under-weight, headaches, shortness of breath, etc.
13. Children on probation need more intensive and effective casework by the probation officers.
14. A child needs supervision when parents are working and the child is not in school.
15. Children need understanding and love but also firm and consistent discipline from those in authority.
16. Problem children often need group therapy and counseling. Often parents need therapy and counseling also.
17. Family counseling is often needed or at certain intervals and sometimes on a long-term basis.
18. Training and education of parents are often needed in the areas of child care, child rearing, truancy, unruliness, alcoholism, financial problems, domestic management, etc.
19. Children need appropriate clothing and shoes to enhance their self-image and social relationships. This might require economic aid or employment or better resource management.
20. Children need encouragement to accept themselves. They often need reassurance and help in getting over

the, often, early erroneous assumption that others are o.k. and that they are not o.k.

21. Children need information regarding personal hygiene.

1. Personal cleanliness and good grooming help to promote the personality and develop personal pride.

22. Children need exposure to spiritual and moral training and influence, such as a church, church school, citizenship training classes and wisely taught sex education. This will provide them with sounder bases for making moral judgments according to the moral values and expected standards of society.

23. The ability to read and write is vital to wholesome self-development and positive self-expression. Remedial tutoring should be mandatory for some children.

24. Schools should revise their academic curriculum to meet the actual needs of the various achievement and performance levels of students in a realistic way.

25. Many children would benefit from vocational training and/or work-training programs.

26. All communities need well planned and adequately staffed leisure time programs geared to provide opportunities for meaningful use of talents and satisfying achievements.

27. A child needs involvement in some type of activity in which he can excel. He needs to have his talents discovered, encouraged and developed.

28. Methods and means should be developed to give children a feeling of success about something important to them as individuals to stimulate positive personal growth.

29. A child needs realistic hope and realistic goals determined partly by the child.
30. Children need positive reinforcements for their successes rather than being constantly bombarded with negative criticism.
31. Children need rewards and reinforcements for good behavior and compliments on a job well done.
32. The community resources, to meet the multiple needs of problem children and families, should be developed and coordinated for ready availability and accessibility.
33. Many children are in need of the "mainstream" cultural exposures that exist outside of their confined and limited sub-groups and sub-cultures.
34. Children need membership in groups that provide a feeling of belongingness and a strong sense of positive group identification, such as school clubs, boys' clubs, girls' clubs, scouting, YMCA, church and other neighborhood clubs.
35. Children need to develop communication skills in order to express themselves more properly and develop social literacy.
36. Children need supportive, goal-oriented and humane structures that are so conceived and conditioned as to maximize the development of their potential and encourage the full expression of their personalities.

CHAPTER 14
EDUCATION AND EMPOWERMENT OF YOUTH

Foundations for Spiritual Recovery

The pastoral addiction counselor must be aware and knowledgeable of certain information, procedures, sequences and resources to be effective in the recovery process. The following is a general guideline for that effort:

1. Must have basic pharmacological knowledge of drug use, abuse, dependence and addiction. Must have an understanding of the concepts of drug use, abuse, dependence and addiction.
2. Must be knowledgeable of the predictable consequences of drug abuse and addiction in the following areas:
   A. Medical (physical and psychological)
   B. Personal and social
   C. Ethical and spiritual
3. Learn how to evaluate, assess and provide the appropriate DSMIV diagnosis and number. Learn how to write a plan for prevention, treatment and recovery.
4. Learn the dynamics of alcohol and other drug withdrawal syndrome. Learn the distinction and rationale for ambulatory and inpatient detoxification.
5. Be knowledgeable of the community resources of help for the appropriate areas of need, such as

medical, social, economical, housing, employment, ethical and spiritual, etc.

6. Learn the clinical skills of providing individual, group, family, crisis and intervention counseling, appropriate referral and case management services.
7. Learn the skills in providing motivation, inspiration, community support systems and a sustained commitment to spiritual recovery.
8. The pastoral must have a resource of educational and spiritual sound principles and doctrines for teaching and guidance. The pastoral counselor must be an advocate for social justice and educational and economic opportunities.

The Christian Institute or Public Theology
Suggested Monthly Training Seminar Schedule

OVERVIEW

Purpose:	To provide education, training and skill development for pragmatic Christian services of young people in community.
Goal:	To develop and utilize the maximum potential of every young person in the community for their spiritual growth and effective Christian service.
Method:	Provide monthly educational and training seminars at some appropriate place in community
For Everyone:	For all interested and appropriate persons.

SUGGESTED SCHEDULE

January:	Series One
	• How to Maintain Good Physical and Mental Health.
	• How to Develop a Popular Personality and Win Friends.
	Series Two: God-Creation – Family - Marriage - Work
	• What is man's place in creation?
	• What is the sacred duty of man?
	• How can we contribute to be a better future for mankind?
	• What is God's purpose for His creation?
February:	Series One:
	• Utilizing Knowledge and Inspiration from the Past.
	• Negro History - Black Heroes – A Proud Heritage.
	Series Two: People – Community – Government – Nations
	• Education and inspiration from the past.
	• How can universal brotherhood be accomplished?
	• How can we restore safety, health and beauty to our community?

March:	Series One:
	• Assertion Skills Training
	• Learn How to Ask, Seek and Knock for the fulfillment of your needs.
	Series Two: The Resources of God
	• What is responsible stewardship of God's resources?
	• Who is responsible for stewardship?
	• How does God want us to use, distribute and share His resources?
April:	Series One:
	• Alcohol and Drug Education.
	• Learn About the Dynamics of Chemical Dependence.
	• How to Avoid the Traps of Substance Abuse and Drug Addiction.
	Series Two: Fruitful Living – The Abundant Life
	• Why does mankind need salvation?
	• What is the Mission of the Church?
	• What does it mean to live abundantly?
May:	Series One:
	• How to Get a Job.
	• Where and How to Look for a Job.

	• The Application – The Resume – Interview – Appearance.
	• Survival Strategy.
	Series Two: Sharing Human Values
	• What is the value of love?
	• The three eternal values – goodness, truth and beauty.
	• What is God's role for women?
	• What is the duty of responsible motherhood?
	• How can personal relationships be enhanced?
June:	Series One:
	• How to Develop Effective Communication Skills.
	• How to Listen – How to Be Attentive.
	• How to Identify Feelings – How to Examine Content – How to Respond.
	Series Two: Cultivating Healthy and Wholesome Relationships Between Men and Women
	• What is God's role for men?
	• How can healthy social relationships between men and women be enhanced?
	• What is the true function of Marriage?
	• How can mutual respect between men and women be improved?

July:	Series One:
	• How to Build a Positive Self Image and Self Confidence.
	• Self-Actualization – Self Esteem – Self Acceptance.
	• How to Know That You Are O.K.
	Series Two: The Kingdom of God – On Earth – In Heaven
	• What is the meaning of Democratic Government in a Christian Society?
	• What is the meaning of Freedom? Justice? Equality?
	• What are universal human rights?
	• How can we improve the protection of our civil constitutional and human rights?
August:	Series One:
	• How to Succeed in School.
	• How to Learn About Scholarship Opportunities, Financial Assistance, Educational Loans, and Educational Works Programs.
	• What is Education and Its Value to You?
	Series Two: Self Actualization
	• How can we become what we were meant to be?
	• How can we develop our potentials and fulfill our dreams?
	• What is our obligation to the development of others?

September:	Series One:
	• Human Relationship – Courtship – Marriage – Family.
	• Problems of Black Male/Female Relationships Explored.
	• How the Problems Can Be Minimized and the Relationship Improved.
	Series Two: Jobs – Employment – Money – Wealth – Management
	• How can our jobs and employment be used in the scheme of salvation?
	• How can our money and wealth be used to promote the Kingdom of God?
	• How can we achieve an equitable balance with production, consumption and the distribution of goods and services?
	• What are the principles of effective management?
October:	Series One:
	• How to Manage Emotional Stress.
	• How to Overcome Mental Depression.
	• How to Use Time Wisely, Live and Enjoy the Abundant Life.
	Series Two: The Power of Faith
	• How can faith be revitalized for the survival and good for mankind.

	• What is the relationship of faith to fellowship, friendship and liberation?
	• What is the role of faith in human progress?
	• Why is the power of faith so vital for the human race?
November:	Series One:
	• Assertive Training.
	• How to Speak, Act and Express Thoughts and Feelings with More Self Confidence and Courage.
	• How to Speak Up for Self.
	Series Two: The Need for Human Services
	• How to assess vital human needs?
	• Prerequisites for providing human needs.
	• How to help those in need.
	• How can we determine that we are providing something of value?
December:	Series One:
	• Learn the Art and Science of Christian Counseling.
	• The Process – Techniques – Principles.
	Series Two: Receiving and Giving Gifts
	• What are the benefits of giving?
	• How can the value of gifts be assessed?
	• How can give to redeem and provide salvation?

	• How can we give without demeaning?
	• The relationship of giving to friendship and fellowship.
	• Relationship between gift, giver and receiver.

Foundation Principles of Success for Young People

1. You are a special and unique human being. Be thankful you are special. Rejoice in your uniqueness. Use your uniqueness in creative ways to improve yourself to make a better-civilized humanity.

2. You are an American. Embrace your Americanism. You have a birthright in America. America is your country. It is your national home. America is a country of freedom and opportunity. Often, more often than not, these opportunities are not given to you. They are available for you. You must prepare yourself to take advantage of the available opportunities. You must be diligent and assertive in taking full advantage of the available opportunities. More aggressive people may even take opportunities that are available for you. These opportunities in America are up for grabs. The competition is stiff. You are an American. Work hard and be intentional in fulfilling your dreams.

3. In order to be motivated to work hard, you must choose a "Success Identify." You must Identify with success, not with failure. You must choose to be a "Winner." Be a competitor. Be an overcomer. Be a fixer. Be a Survivor. Be a Champion. Be a long distance runner. You are going to run into opposition. You are

going to encounter People who do not want you to succeed. Do not give up. Hold on and hold out. Be a Good soldier. Fight the good fight. Keep the Faith.

4. Choose and develop your best self. Only you can become the person that you want to be. Remember, you become what you admire; you become what you aspire to be. You have the power to choose and decide what and who you want to be. You make your own decisions. Choose wisely. Human nature is flexible. It is like wet clay. It can be shaped and formed in a variety of ways. It is your decision. Only your decision to choose to be the best person and the best self that you can count towards who you become.

5. Invest in the future. Prepare and plan for future success. Don't gamble with your future. Set lofty goals. Work hard and work smart to reach those goals. The mark of a high-class person is that they are oriented toward the future. They don't live just for today. They invest in the future.

6. Be aware of the new and developing technology. Technology can be used for good or bad. It can be used to make life better or worse. These cell phones are handy, but they can also be disruptive. There is even talk of putting microchips under the skin to track or reveal certain information about you. Be aware of DNA. Be aware of your DNA. Be aware of where you leave your DNA. It can be used to help or hurt you.

7. God has revealed himself, his Will, his Way, his Wisdom, his Standards, his Works and his Love in human history. It is the responsibility of each individual to learn for himself or herself, this historical revelation of God in our history. No one else can make

your God's decision for you. You must decide on God for yourself.

8. There is a moral law that says, "You Reap What You Sow." Therefore, give the world the best that you have, and the best will come back to you. You get back what you send out. Send out good things. Good things will come back to you. For the same reason, if you send out bad things, bad things will come back to you. Sow good seeds and you will reap good fruit.

9. To be successful you must develop a consistent and persistent work ethic. You must not waste your time. You must not sleep it away, daydream it away or play it away. You must work hard, and you must work smart. You must work to be the best.

In the words of Dr. Benjamin E. Mays, who was President of Morehouse College for 27 years: "You must do your job so well, that no man living and no man dead, and no man yet to be born can do that job any better."

The Public Theology Association

This is a generic proposal for the establishment of a student organization on the campus of colleges and other educational institutions (and under their respective authorities) known as The Public Theology Association.

Purpose of the Organization

The purpose of this voluntary student organization is to learn about public theology and to promote its precepts of academic excellence/achievement, religious/spiritual/ethical values, human health, social advancement, cultural enrichment, economic and leadership development. The purpose is to provide an opportunity for students to learn about the most noble values and ideals known to humanity and a means to summon the faith and the courage to practice them for the public and the common good.

Some Core Objectives

1. Explore the role and values of public theology based on sound biblical and religious doctrines.
2. Reflections on biblical foundations for improving the quality of life, security of civilization and guidance for the success and triumph of humanity.
3. Learn how to apply religious creeds, ethical and spiritual values to motivate positive attitudes, ethical behavior and responsible living for the common good.
4. Learn how to incorporate the spiritual (biblical) domain of learning in education along with the cognitive, affective and psychomotor learning domains.
5. To explore ethical and moral foundations for cooperative and constructive living in a cultural diverse, heterogeneous and religious pluralistic society.
6. Develop an appreciation for the historical, social, cultural and universal role of the Judeo-Christian religion in America and the world.
7. Explore the role of public theology in American history, Black American history, the Civil Rights movement and as the guardian of truth, social justice,

liberty, freedom, Democracy, the way and the witness of God in earth and the Universe.

Student Success Alliance

Purpose

To host a youth forum to create ongoing organizations for the attainment of optimum student success and development in high schools and possibly college.

Proposed Mission Statement

Create and maintain such school conditions, teaching and learning environment, that will afford and inspire the optimum opportunity for the attainment for every student; the maximum academic achievement, character and leadership development, responsible, ethical and moral conduct, noble, aesthetic, cultural and spiritual values.

Proposed Goals

1. Increase academic achievement and other educational student-related performances above the National standards.
2. Increase significantly, the percentage of students who remain in school and graduate with increased grade point averages, high honors, recognitions, awards and scholarships and college admissions.
3. Create a new pride in personal appearance with an emphasis on dressing for success and respect.

4. Create a new renaissance school spirit of pride with a positive atmosphere of courtesy and respect. Adapt the school song that will express this new school spirit or write a new inspiring school song that will inspire the spirit of the school for elevated thoughts, higher goals, unity, increased motivation and a purpose of noble significance.
5. Decrease and eliminate school dropouts, delinquent, disruptive and negative attitudes and behaviors.
6. Inspire and motivate every student to actualize their God-given potential for success and greatness.

Case Management Empowerment

Remedial, Preventive and Growth Service Needs

	1.	Food, Shelter, Clothing
	2.	A Living Environment of Safety and Security
	3.	Health Services and Personal Care
	4.	Employment and Financial Security
	5.	Human Support Services and Fellowship
	6.	Education and Training Opportunities
	7.	Transportation
	8.	Computer and Internet Access
	9.	Religious and Fellowship Experience
	10.	Recreational and Peaceful Leisure Time

Some Barriers to Human Services

	1.	Physical Barriers
	2.	Psychological Barriers
	3.	Socioeconomic Barriers
	4.	Educational and Technological Barriers
	5.	Racial, Class and Ethnic Barriers
	6.	Age, Religious and Sex Barriers
	7.	Geographical, Language and Cultural Barriers
	8.	Legal, Political and Discriminatory Barriers
	9.	Unethical, Immoral, Unprofessional and Criminal Barriers
	10.	Negligence, Passive, Uncaring and Indifference Barriers

Case Management Services

	1.	Link the Client's needs to the available services
	2.	Remove barriers that prevent service and resources to clients
	3.	Identify and create needed support services for disadvantaged clients
	4.	Be aggressive in cutting through administrative and bureaucratic red tape for clients
	5.	Create Support Systems for the helpless, homeless, hungry and hopeless
	6.	Become a Bold and Consistent Advocate for Disadvantaged Clients/Persons
	7.	Create Policies and Systems to Motivate, Inspire and Empower the Disadvantaged

	8.	Create Directories of Community Resources and Referral Agencies for the Disadvantaged
	9.	Connect Clients to Community Agencies and Fellowship Groups for Spiritual Growth
	10.	Connect Clients with Agencies that Educate and Nurture the Human Spirit for Growth, Success, Self-Reliance and Resilience

CHAPTER 15
DIRECTIONS FOR TREATMENT AND HEALING

Effective Treatment Methods and Approaches for Restoration

1. Children must have supervision and guidance from well adjusted, mentally healthy, emotionally stable and morally sound adults. The health of the caseworker is his greatest asset in therapeutic relationships. The caseworker not only prescribes remedies, but he himself must be a vital part of that prescription. He must develop a healing relationship, and administer health where there is sickness, knowledge where there is ignorance and love where there is hatred.

2. Accept the child's way of living with a non-threatening and nonjudgmental attitude, and never approach him or his family with a "holier than thou" attitude.

3. Adjust your approach and communication to the child's level of comprehension and interest. Tune in on the child's "wavelength." Try to see things from his perspective.

4. Encourage and compliment the child whenever possible; accentuate his positive points to boost his self-concept and reinforce positive behavior.

5. Be a good listener to the juvenile's problems and be completely honest and fair in dealing with him.

6. Try to upgrade the juvenile's self-esteem and encourage the social mobility of his family.
7. Help the child to find success in some areas and extend it to other areas. Help him to get in the habit of legitimate success and achievement.
8. The caseworker's concern should be extended to every phase of the juvenile's life, and he be given frequent guidance and counseling.
9. Practical and appropriate behavior modification techniques help change maladaptive behavior and develop positive attitudes toward socially acceptable behavior.
10. The juvenile must be persuaded to understand early, the penalty and continuous social costs associated with the stigma of crime and delinquency. Delinquency does not pay the delinquent—it costs him his most cherished rights and valuable possessions.
11. Behavior modification contracts and a meaningful behavior modification program with the worker having a low manageable caseload is conducive for treatment.
12. Consistent checks on the child's behavior in the home, school and neighborhood. Final conclusions must not be made until the child's story is told and a personal investigation is made concerning reports of others.
13. Small group talk sessions, group therapy and guided group interaction can be very helpful treatment methods if conducted properly.
14. Periodic follow-up counseling, including the parents at home and the teacher or counselor at school.

15. A strong meaningful one to one relationship between the child and his probation officer with frequency.
16. Establish a workable relationship with the child and his family and make self-available to them when necessary, and especially during a crisis.
17. Refer the parents to the appropriate community resources to meet their needs and encourage them to assume increasing responsibility for their own welfare.
18. Perform diagnostic studies to determine the source of trouble in the home and help the parents resolve those problems that have contributed to the child's delinquency. In some cases, professional family counseling may be necessary.
19. When necessary, use volunteer services such as VPOs and big brothers and sisters to intensify and individualize probation services.
20. Interest the child in social, moral and religious activities in the neighborhood, church, school or other similar activities and agencies.
21. Involve the child in camp activities, and visits to historical sites, amusement parks and play lands.
22. Help the child to develop home pride and community pride by getting him involved in home projects and community projects such as cleaning, or other projects to beautify, repair, make more comfortable and enrich the surroundings in which he lives.
23. Secure more beneficial educational, vocational and employment opportunities for the child, such as youth corps, job corps, Street Academy, special classes, schools, courses, etc.
24. Use referrals to the proper community resources such as drug clinics, mental health clinics, medical, dental

and eye clinics and others when deemed necessary and beneficial. Health problems frequently contribute to children's lack of achievement and their maladaptive behavior.

25. Every probation plan should include well defined goals. The child should understand clearly what is expected of him by the probation officer and parents. Be firm and consistent.

26. Detention for recidivists can be used in conjunction with reality therapy and behavior modification, provided the goal in detention is planned and supervised treatment, and not arbitrary punishment with automatic detention periods.

27. Use reality therapy approach in counseling, thus teaching child to accept responsibility for his behavior and the consequences of his decisions and actions.

28. The child should be so guided in his reasoning so that he develops a high degree of self-awareness, self-discipline and self-responsibility, so that he will be capable of making those decisions which are in the best interest of himself and society.

29. The child must be taught or conditioned to develop empathy— the ability to sympathize, to imagine himself in another's place, and to feel their feelings and share their thoughts.

30. The community, through its institutions, organization, activities and the quality of its environment, must be designed and enriched so as to contribute to the health and adjustment of maladaptive persons.

31. Always maintain an optimistic attitude and never communicate to the child that you have lost faith in him. Because a child will try to live up to the expectation of adults who place trust in him.

32. Involve the child in youth guidance programs geared toward cooperative work and play. Such programs often teach children how to get along with others, respect authority, feel a sense of accomplishment and establish a goal in life.

33. The community should provide more temporary group homes, foster homes, halfway houses and daycare centers as alternatives to detention and long-term incarceration.

34. A noncoercive agency such as a youth services bureau should be developed to deal with unruly children and other problems of youth which cannot and perhaps should not be handled by a court.

35. The community must make available more vocational programs for the mentally retarded or slow learners, remedial reading programs, work release and youth job programs and other programs designed to meet special needs.

36. More community based intensive care programs are needed to deal with family counseling and management; to rehabilitate homes as opposed to removing a child from the home; to help educate families of the existence and the utilization of community resources.

37. Transactional analysis has the potential of becoming a very effective treatment method in psychotherapy and in helping the client to use the particular ego state which offers the most appropriate response social actions.

Keys to Reality Therapy

1. Involvement
The therapist involves himself with the child. He uses praise, approval, and reward. He might pat the child on the back or shoulder to indicate friendship or approval. The therapist is warm, friendly and subjective.

2. Reveals Himself
The therapist reveals himself to the child. He might do this by sharing with the child personal references about himself. He shares his humanness with the child.

3. "I" and "Me" Communication
The therapist communicates with the frequent use of "I" and "Me" to personalize and intensify the relationship.

4. Concentrate on Here and Now
The therapist does not deal with the child's history or psychological diagnosis. The emphasis is on the present situation and circumstances.

5. Concentrate on Behavior
Don't concentrate on feelings and attitude. Do not share bad feelings. Concentrate on outside behavior and not thoughts, feelings or attitude. Proper conduct is the goal. A child has a right to his feelings, thoughts and attitude without being threatened or having these private and personal components of his being invaded.

6. Ask What-Not Why

"What" focuses on a specific. "Why" requires the kind of reflection which might be irrelevant to the problem at hand.

7. Have Child Evaluate What He Did

Is it doing you any good? Who did it help? Was it a good idea? Was that the best course of action?

8. After Evaluation - Help Child Work Out a Plan

The plan should be modest which assures success. It should be within the child's capability.

9. Follow a Plan with a Contract

Negotiate a contract with child. Make sure child feels that it is fair and within his capability.

10. Accept No Excuse

Child must live up to the contract or abide by the consequences. Real life does not excuse.

11. Work in Groups

Children can change each other, and they can give strength and support to each other in groups.

12. Use Praise, Reward, Humanness, Touch

13. Don't Press Too Hard

Immediate results might not be forth coming. Be firm. but also, be patient and understanding.

14. Don't Give Up

Human nature can change. Minds can change.
They often do. Never give up on a child. If you believe he can
and he believes he can—he can.

Proposal for Providing Character Education in Schools

The character education described in this proposal is based on the Character Education Program that was signed into Georgia law by Governor Roy Barnes on April 23, 1999. The law mandated that all schools in Georgia from K-12 incorporate character education into the school educational curriculum. The components of this Character Education Law include 27 specific enumerated character traits as follows: cheerfulness, citizenship, compassion, cleanliness, cooperation, courtesy, courage, creativity, diligence, fairness, generosity, honesty, kindness, loyalty, patriotism, patience, perseverance, punctuality, respect for the Creator, respect for others, respect for the environment, self-respect, self-control, sportsmanship, school pride, temperance, tolerance.

These character traits are designed to assist, teach, motivate and inspire students, in a comprehensive way, to develop positive attitudes, responsible behavior, ethical principles, ethical practice, successful identities, academic achievement, cultural enrichment, personal health, peace and goodwill toward others as patriotic American citizens. These character traits will help the students to focus on the seriousness of educational achievement, the sacredness of life, the optimum use of time, personal development, moral and spiritual growth. The students will have the opportunity to learn about the great values of freedom, justice and equality that moved civilization toward peace, prosperity and democratic self-governing community living. These character traits are designed to help the students to develop autonomous self-governing and individual responsibility for personal behavior determined voluntarily internally as opposed to outside external involuntary enforcement. It is the expectation and hope that this character education experience will help the students to get more seriously on the time-tested validated tracks of successful living through true science, true art, true law and true religion.

This proposal is to be accomplished through trained volunteers with valid certifications to provide the above services in conjunction with the respective schools according to the guidelines, policies and procedures of the respective school. These services are to be provided to a selected number of students (between six to twelve students) in a suitable space at the school for one-hour sessions, for once or twice each week. One or two qualified volunteers from the Faith-Based Organization will lead the Character Education Group. The finalized agreement will be worked out with the designated persons from the Faith-Based Organization and the Respective School where the educational and group service is to be provided.

Fundamental Traits for Character Education

The Consistent practice of the following Character traits enhances Career success in life. (Georgia Law 20-2-145)

1.	Cheerfulness	Be pleasant and encouraging.
2.	Citizenship	Be a responsible member of society
3.	Compassion	Develop a caring and positive concern for others.
4.	Cleanliness	Practice personal environmental cleanliness.
5.	Cooperation	Learn and Practice teamwork.
6.	Courtesy	Extend friendliness and hospitality to others.
7.	Courage	Be brave. Take a stand for the right thing.
8.	Creativity	Use your intelligence to think/make new things.
9.	Diligence	Don't give up. Hold on. Endure to the end.
10.	Fairness	Treat all with respect. Give everyone their dues.
11.	Generosity	Develop a spirit of giving and sharing.
12.	Honesty	Be real, bonafide, sincere, true.
13.	Kindness	Be pleasant, affirming, helpful and positive.

14.	Loyalty	Be reliable, dependable, and committed.
15.	Patriotism	Express care and concern for your country/nation.
16.	Patience and Virtue	Wait with hope and endurance.
17.	Perseverance	Work with hope and endurance.
18.	Punctuality	Be on time or ahead of time.
19.	Respect for the Creator	Reverence for God of the universe.
20.	Respect for others	Human life and human rights are sacred.
21.	Respect for environment	Keep clean, safe and healthy.
22.	Self-Respect	Keep your integrity. Be the best you can be.
23.	Self-Control	Let wisdom, knowledge and responsibility guide you.
24.	Sportsmanship	Play fairly. Lose gracefully. You are a winner.
25.	School Pride	Help your school achieve it's goal by achieving yours.
26.	Temperance	Keep your mind, emotions and actions balance with reality.
27.	Tolerance	Be understanding and considerate of those who do not meet your expectations.

The above character traits were abstracted from Georgia Law 20-2-145 and adapted by Foundation Baptist Church, Inc. to be used to teach character education in schools and other educational and human services facilities. Atlanta, GA (Feb. 15, 2013)

From Addiction and Darkness to Spiritual Light

PREQUISITES FOR SPIRITUAL HEALING & WELLNESS

The journey to spiritual healing and wholeness requires the following conditions and avenues of expression:

	Something Noble and Significant to Believe in.
	A validated truth that is dependable and trustworthy.
	A value of significance that offers hope and is worthy of embracing.
	A High Calling from God that merits unconditional surrender and ultimate allegiance.

PRESCRIPTIONS FOR HEALING AND RECOVERY

The Prescriptions for Healing and Recovery require certain conditions, attitudes and actions. The following is a general sequence of attitudes, conditions and actions for the journey to Spiritual Healing and Wholeness.

1. An enlightened personal awareness and self-discovery.
2. An informed social and environmental awareness of the world of reality.
3. Enlightened personal, situational and circumstantial awareness.
4. A self-searching personal reflection and introspection.
5. A reverent acknowledgment of reality, the love and the power of God.
6. An analytical and prayerful exploration of options and directions to fruition, recovery and fulfillment.
7. Institute a comprehensive assessment of resources and support systems.
8. Adopt internal resolutions with mental and spiritual preparations.
9. Initiate an act of repentance and forgiveness of self and others.
10. Initiate liberating activities from the bondage of the past.
11. Embrace the survival values for successful and triumphant living.
12. Claim a personal spiritual identity rooted in the Word, Ways and Will of God.
13. Receive the infusion of faith, hope, love, truth and courage through study, prayer, meditation, worship and fellowship.
14. Continue to seek truth, knowledge wisdom, understanding and their redemptive application in the will of God.
15. Identify and pursue specific missions, causes and purposes for living a meaningful abundant life for self and others.

16. Establish specific redemptive and salvation goals to edify humanity and glorify God.
17. Establish a dedicated focus on the mission, methods and goals to be accomplished.
18. Develop a resolute and unwavering commitment to the cause and the high calling of God of which you have been commissioned.
19. Make investments for personal, intellectual, spiritual, educational and economic growth for uplifting humanity and for future returns.
20. Pursue goals of self-actualization, social redemption and human salvation.

The pursuit of spiritual healing and wholeness is a continuous process. It must become a way of life. The above prerequisites and prescriptions for healing and recovery must be inculcated in our pattern of living and the core of our being.

MEANS OF CULTURAL TRANSFORMATION

1.	Reflection:	Assessment of cultural change, meditate on cultural conditions and options available for transformation
2.	Repentance:	Confess genuine sorrow and guilt for years of neutrality, indifference, missed opportunities, forfeitures and failures.
3.	Forgiveness:	Petition God for forgiveness for neglecting the health of the family, the church, the community, the culture, the nation and society

4.	Fellowship:	Join spiritual group for unity, knowledge, understanding, wisdom, growth, support, direction, resources and service
5.	Theological/ Biblical Study:	Regular study of the inspired Word of God and theological knowledge passed down through centuries for the ultimate salvation of humankind. It is knowledge beyond culture.
6.	Mind Renewal:	Embrace the Gospel enlightenment of Truth, the Light, the Way, wisdom, Holy Spirit and the mind of Christ.
7.	Rebirth:	Conversion, regeneration, New Nature, New Creature, rededication, new resolve, new commitment, Born Again, New beginning with God.
8.	Socialization:	Teach and practice survival values and sound doctrines through the institutions of society. Teach and practice the ways of righteousness and social justice and freedom. Teach and encourage respect for the person, property and rights of others. Teach and practice reverence for God, God's creation and the sacredness of human life.
9.	Redemption:	Rising above secular, material and temporal values. Rising above mundane, humanistic and idolatrous values.

		Reaching heights of noble significance and eternal merits.
10.	Transcendence:	A power that goes beyond and exceeds the natural powers of the world. It is the ultimate omnipotent power from above. A power beyond creation without limitations.
11.	Educational Competence:	Keeping pace with current relevant knowledge for intelligent and wise actions.
12.	Commission:	Authorized methods and strategies to carry out the mission of cultural transformation.

FOOTNOTES

1. Maude M. Craig and Laila A. Budd, "The Juvenile Offender-Recidivism and Companions." Crime and Delinquency, Vol. 13, No. 2. (April 1967), pp. 346-347.
2. Sol Rubin, "Recidivism and Recidivism Statistics," National Probation and Parole Association Journal, Vol. 4, No. 3 (July 1958), p.333.
3. Norval Morris, The Habitual Criminal. (London: University of London Press, 1951), p. 3.
4. Ibid., p. 3.
5. H. M. Metcalf, "Recidivism and The Courts," Journal of Criminal Law and Criminology, Vol. 26, No. 3, p. 367, as quoted by Norval Morris, The Habitual Criminal, (London: University of London Press, 1951), p. 3.
6. Ruth Shonie Cavan, Criminology, (New York: Thomas Y. Crowell Company, 1956), pp. 107-108.
7. Louis Berlin, "Adolescent Recidivism," National Probation and Parole Association Journal, Vol. 4 (July 1968), p. 276.
8. Ibid., p.276.
9. John W. Mannering, "Significant Characteristics of Recidivists," National Probation and Parole Association Journal, Vol. 12 (October 1966), p. 216.
10. Charles B. Thompson, "A Psychiatric Study of Recidivists," American Journal of Psychiatry, (November 1937), p. 591.
11. David C. Twain, "Current Research Related to Crime and Delinquency," Federal Probation, Vol. XXX (March 1966), p. 48.

12. Arthur Jaffee and Alice Reed, "Jamming the Revolving Door," Federal Probation, Vol. XXIII (December 1969), p. 32.

13. 30 Morton and Lucia White, The Intellectual Versus The City (New York: The New American Library, Inc., 1962), p. 153.

14. Ibid., p. 21.

15. Dugald S. Arbuckle and Lawrence Litwack, "A Study of Recidivism among Juvenile Delinquents," Federal Probation, Vol. XXIV (December 1960), p. 45.

16. Ibid., p. 48.

17. Ibid., p. 48.

18. Alexander Van West, "Cultural Background and Treatment of the Persistent Offender," Federal Probation, Vol. XXVIII (June 1964), p.18.

19. Ibid., p. 18.

20. Ibid., p. 19.

21. President's Commission on Law Enforcement and Administration of Justice, "The Challenge of Crime is a Free Society," Washington, D.C.: Government Printing Office 1967, p. 57, as quoted by Sterling Tucker, "The Ghetto, the Ghettoized, and Crime," Federal Probation, Vol. XXIII (September 1969), p. 5.

22. Sterling Tucker, "The Ghetto, The Ghettoized, and Crime," Federal Probation, Vol. XXXIII (September 1969).

23. Julius Horwitz, "The Arithmetic of Delinquency," The New Light on Juvenile Delinquency, (New York: The H. W. Wilson Company, 1967), p. 18.

24. Donald J. Tyrell, "Why Can't We Understand Juvenile Delinquency, Federal Probation, Vol. XXVIII (June 1964), pp. 21-22.

25. Juvenile Court Act of 1951, as amended through 1968, 1968 Session of the General Assembly, (Acts 1951, pp. 291, 293; 1956, pp. 69, 70; 1968, pp. 1013; Ga. Code Ann. Section 24-2401).

26. David Easton, A Framework for Political Analysis (Englewood Cliffs: Prentice Hall, 1965).

27. Martin Greenberg, "A Concept of Community," Journal of the National Association of Social Workers, Vol. 19 (January 1974), p. 64.

28. Ibid., p. 64.

29. Claude S. George, Jr. The History of Management Thought (Englewood Cliffs: Prentice-Hall, Inc., 1968), p. 178.

30. Morton and Lucia White, The Intellectual Versus The City (New York: The New American Library, Inc., 1962), p. 153.

31. Ibid., p. 151.

32. Walter C. Reckless, The Crime Problem (New York: Appleton-Century-Crofts, Inc., 1961), pp. 55-56.

33. Description and Evaluation of Neighborhood Centers, For the Office of Economic Opportunity. Contract No. OEO-1257. (Albuquerque: Kirschner Associates, 1966), p. 2.

34. Robert M. Carter, Probation, Parole and Community Corrections (New York: J. Wiley, 1976), p. 503.

35. Bertram S. Griggs and Gary R. McCune, "Community-Based Correctional Programs: A Survey and Analysis," Federal Probation, Vol. 36 (June 1972), p. 11.

36. Ibid., p. 9.

37. Joe Hudson and Others, "Diversion Programming in Criminal Justice: The Case of Minnesota," Federal Probation, Vol. 39 (March 1975), p. 12.

38. Ibid., p. 15.

39. Ibid., p. 15.

40. Kenneth F. Schoen, "Port: A New Concept of Community-Based Correction," Federal Probation, Vol. 36 (September 1972), pp. 35-40.

41. Ted Palmer, "The Youth Authority's Community Treatment Project," Federal Probation, Vol. 38 (March 1974), p. 3.

42. Ibid., p. 7.

43. W. H. Pearce, "Community-Based Treatment of Offenders in England," Federal Probation, Vol. 38 (March 1974), pp. 47-51.

44. Ibid., pp. 47-48.

45. Clementine L. Kaufman, "Community Service Volunteers: A British Approach to Delinquency Prevention," Federal Probation, Vol. 37 (December 1973), p. 36.

46. Ibid., p. 36.

47. Hudson, "Diversion Programming in Criminal Justice," p.19.

48. Carter, Probation Parole and Community, p. 489.

49. Ibid., pp. 494-497.

50. Alvin W. Cohn, "The Failure of Correctional Management.* Crime and Delinquency, NCCD Vol. 19 (July 1973). p. 323.

51. Ibid., p. 329.

52. Robert E. Keldgord and Robert O. Horris, "New Directions for Corrections," Federal Probation, Vol. 36 (March 1972). pp. 3-7.

53. Francis J. Bridges and Others. Management Decisions and Organizational Policy: Text, Cases and Incidents (Boston: Allyn and Bacon, Inc., 1971), p. 67.

54. William I. Goodman and Eric G. Freund, Principles and Practice of Urban Planning (Washington, D.C. International City Manager's Association, 1968), p. 3.

55. Edward S. Greenberg, "The Consequences of Worker Participation," Social Science Quarterly, Vol. 56, (September 1975), p. 192.

56. Carl F. Goodman, "Public Employment and the Supreme Court's 1975-76 Term," Journal of the International Personnel Management Association, Vol. 55 (Sept-Oct, 1976), pp. 287-301.

57. F. Arnold McDermott, "Merit Systems Under Fire," Journal of the Personnel Management Association, Vol. 5 (Sept.-Oct. 1976), p. 226.

58. Ronald M. Pavalko, Sociology of Occupations and Professions. (Itasca, Illinois: F. E. Peacock Publishers, Inc., 1971), pp. 51-52.

59. Edmund P. Learned and others, Business Policy: Text and Cases (Homewood, Illinois: Richard D. Irwin, Inc., 1969), p.3.

60. Harold Koontz and Cyril O'Donnell, Principles of Management: An Analysis of Managerial Functions (New York: McGraw-Hill Book Company, 1968), p. 5.

61. Claude S. George, Jr. The History of Management Thought (Englewood Cliffs: Prentice-Hall, Inc., 1968). pp. 162-171.

62. Willie James Webb, God's Spiritual Prescriptions for Healing, Liberation and Salvation and The Way Out of Darkness: Vital Public Theology

BIBLIOGRAPHY

BOOKS

Abrahamsen, David, The Psychology of Crime. New York: John Wiley and Sons, Inc., 1960.

Alexander, Frans, and Healey, William. Roots of Crime. New York: Alfred Knopf, 1935.

Bagdikian, Ben H. and Dash, Leon. The Shame of the Prisons. New York: The Washington Post Company, 1972.

Beach, Dale S. Managing People at Work: Readings in Personnel. New York: The MacMillan Company, 1971.

Bonger, William. Criminality and Economic Conditions. Boston: Little, Brown, and Company, 1916.

Brasel, Boris. The Elements of Crime. New Jersey: Patterson Smith, 1969.

Brawley, Edward Allen. Community and Social Service Education in the Community College: Issues and Characteristics. New York: Council on Social Work Education, 1972.

Breckinridge, Sophonisba P., and Abbot, Edith. The Delinquent Child and the Home. New York: Russell Sage Foundation, 1912.

Bridges, Francis J.; Olm, Kenneth W.; Barnhill, J. Allison. Management Decisions and Organizational Policy: Text, Cases and Incidents. Boston: Allyn and Bacon, Inc., 1971.

Carkhuff, Robert R. The Art of Helping: An Introduction to Life Skills. Washington, D.C.: Human Resource Development Press, Inc., 1973.

Carter, Robert Melvin. Probation, Parole and Community Corrections. New York: John Wiley, 1976.

Cavan, Ruth Shonle. Criminology. New York: Thomas Y. Cromwell Company, 1956.

Cloward, Richard A., and Olin, Lloyd E. Delinquency and Opportunity. New York: The Free Press, 1960.

Community Action Studies Project: Action Planning for Community Health Services. A Report. Washington Public Affairs Press, 1967.

Description and Evaluation of Neighborhood Centers. For the Office of Economic Opportunity. Contract No. OEO-1257. Albuquerque: Kirschner Associates, 1966.

Easton, David. A Framework for Political Analysis. Englewood Cliffs: Prentice-Hall, 1965.

Fantini, Mario D. Decentralization: Achieving Reform. New York: Praeger, 1973.

Farmer, Richard N. Management in the Future. Belmont, California: Wadsworth Publishing Company, Inc., 1969.

Fink, Joseph. The Community and the Police-Conflict or Cooperation. New York: J. Wiley, 1974.

Fox, Vernon. Introduction to Corrections. Englewood Cliffs, 1972.

George, Claude S. Jr. The History of Management Thought. Englewood Cliffs: Prentice-Hall, Inc., 1968.

Giallombardo, Rose. Juvenile Delinquency-A Book of Readings. New York: John Wiley and Sons, Inc., 1966.

Glueck, Sheldon and Eleanor. Criminal Careers in Retrospect. New York: Commonwealth Fund, 1943.

Glueck, Sheldon and Eleanor. Delinquents and Non-Delinquents in Perspective. Massachusetts: Harvard University Press, 1968.

Glueck, Sheldon and Eleanor. Predicting Delinquency and Crime. Massachusetts: Harvard University Press, 1959.

Goodman, William I. and Freund, Eric G. Principles and Practice of Urban Planning. Washington, D.C.: International City Manager's Association, 1968.

Gutman, Robert and Popenoe, David. Neighborhood, City, and Metropolis. New York: Random House, 1970.

Hall, Arthur Cleveland. Crime in Relation to Social Progress. New York: Ams Press, 1968.

Healey, William. The Individual Delinquent. Boston: Little, Brown, and Company, 1915.

Hirsch, Travis. Causes of Delinquency. Berkeley and Los Angeles: University of California Press, 1969.

Johnston, Norman: Savitz, Leonard; and Wolfgang, Marvin E. The Sociology of Punishment and Corrections. New York: John Wiley and Sons. 1970.

Koontz. Harold and O'Donnell, Cyril. Principles of Management. New York: McGraw-Hill Book Company, 1968.

Kvaraceus, William Clement. The Community and the Delinquent: Co-Operative Approaches to Preventing and Controlling Delinquency. Yonkers-On-Hudson, N.Y.: World Book Company, 1954.

Learned, Edmund P.: Christensen, C. Roland; Andrews, Kenneth R.; and Guth, William D. Business Policy: Text and Cases. Homewood, Illinois: Richard D. Irwin, Inc., 1969.

MacLeod, Alastair. Recidivism: A Deficiency Disease. Philadelphia: University of Pennsylvania Press, 1965.

Morris, Norval. The Habitual Criminal. London: University of London Press, 1951.

Pavalko, Ronald M. Sociology of Occupations and Professions. Itasca, Illinois: F.E. Peacock Publishers, Inc., 1971.

Reckless, Walter C. The Crime Problem. New York: Appleton-Century-Crofts, Inc., 1961.

Ross, Bernard and Shireman, Charles (ed.). Social Work Practice and Social Justice: Third NASW Professional Symposium. Washington DC.: National Association of Social Workers, 1973.

Screiber, Arthur F.; Gatons, Paul K.; and Clemmer, Richard B. Economics of Urban Problems: An Introduction. Boston: Houghton Mittlin Company, 1971.

Seay, Maurice F. and Associates. Community Education: A Developing Concept. Michigan: Pendell Publishing Company, 1974.

Sellin, Thorsten, and Wolfgang, Marvin E. (ed.). Delinquency— Selected Studies. New York: John Wiley and Sons, Inc., 1969.

Skolnick, Jerome H. and Currie, Elliott. (ed.). Crisis in American Institution. Boston: Little, Brown and Company, 1970.

Solomon, Hassim M. Community Corrections. Boston: Holbrook Press, 1976.

Steel, Ronald, (ed.). New Light on Juvenile Delinquency. New York: H. W. Wilson Company, 1967.

Studt, Elliot. G-Unit: Search for Community in Prison. New York: Russell Sage Foundation, 1968.

The Challenge of Crime in a Free Society: A Report by the President's Commission on Law Enforcement and Administration of Justice. Washington, D.C., U.S. Government Printing Office, Feb. 1967.

The Multi-purpose Senior Centers: A Model Community Action Program. Prepared by the National Council on the Aging for the Community Action Program. Office of Economic Opportunity. New York.

Trojanowicz, Robert C. Community-Based Crime Prevention. Pacific Palisades: Goodyear Publishing Co., 1975.

Webb, Willie James. God's Spiritual Prescriptions for Healing, Liberation and Salvation and The Way Out of Darkness: Vital Public Theology

West, D. J. Present Conduct and Future Delinquency. New York: International University Press, Inc., 1969.

White, Morton and Lucia. The Intellectual Versus the City. New York: The New American Library, Inc., 1962.

Wilson, Robert N. Community Structure and Health Action: A Report on Process Analysis. Washington: Public Affairs Press, 1968.

ARTICLES AND PERIODICALS

Alpander, Guvene G. "Planning Management Training Programs for Organizational Development." Personnel Journal, Vol. 53 (January 1974).

Berlin, Louis. "Adolescent Recidivism," Bates, Fred C. "Recidivism and Rate of Granting Probation," Mannering, John W. "Significant Characteristics of Recidivists," Rubin, Sal. "Recidivism and Recidivism Statistics, "Rector, Milton G. "Factors in Measuring Recidivism as Presented in Annual Reports," Sellin, Thorsten, "Recidivism and Maturation," Turnbaldh, Will C. Association Journal, Vol. 4 (July 1968).

Burdman, Milton. "Realism in Community-Based Correctional Services." Annals of the American Academy of Political and Social Sciences. Vol. 381 (1969).

Burke, Nelson S., and Simmons, Alfred E. "Factors which Precipitate Drop-outs and Delinquency," Federal Probation, Vol. XXIX (March 1965).

Cohn, Alvin W. "The Failure of Correctional Management," Crime and Delinquency, NCCD. Vol. 19 (July 1973).
Craig, Maude, M. and Budd, Leila A. "The Juvenile Offender-Recidivism and Companions," National Council on Crime and Delinquency, Vol. 13 (October 1966).

Georgia Code Ann Section 24-2401. Juvenile Court Act of 1951 as Amended through 1968 by the 1968 Session of the General Assembly of Georgia.

Greenberg. Edward S. "The Consequences of Worker Participation," Social Science Quarterly. Vol. 56 (Sept. 1975). Greenberg, Martin. "A Concept of Community," Journal of the National Association of Social Workers. Vol. 19 (January 1974).

Griggs. Bertram S. and McCune, Gary R. "Community-Based Correctional Programs: A Survey and Analysis," Federal Probation, Vol. 36 (June 1972).

Hudson, Joe. (et al.) "Diversion Programming in Criminal Justice: The Case of Minnesota," Federal Probation, Vol. 39 (March 1975).

Jaffee, Arthur, and Reed, Alice. "Jamming the Revolving Door," Federal Probation, Vol. XXX (September 1969).

Lamb, H. Richard. "A Community Alternative to County Jail: The Hopes and the Realities," Federal Probation, Vol. 39 (March 1975).

Macpherson, David P. "Corrections and the Community." Federal Probation, Vol. 36 (March 1972).

McDermott, F. Arnold. "Merit Systems Under Fire," Journal of the International Personnel Management Association. Vol. 5 (Sept.-Oct. 1976).

Kaufman, Clementine L. "Community Service Volunteers: A British Approach to Delinquency Prevention," Federal Probation, Vol. 37 (December 1973).

Keldgord, Robert E. "New Directions for Corrections," Federal Probation, Vol. 36 (March 1972).

Palmer, Ted. "The Youth Authority's Community Treatment Project," Federal Probation, Vol. 38 (March 1974).

Pettibone, John M. "Community-Based Programs: Catching Up With Yesterday," Federal Probation, Vol. 37 (Sept. 1973).

Pearce. W. H. "Community-Based Treatment of Offenders in England," Federal Probation, Vol. 38 (March 1974).

Rachin, Richard L. "So You Want to Open a Halfway House," Federal Probation, Vol. 36 (March 1972).

Ruhington, Earl. "The 'Revolving Door' Game," National Council on Crime and Delinquency, Vol. 12 (October 1969).

Schoen, Kenneth F. "Port: A New Concept of Community-Based Correction," Federal Probation, Vol. 36 (Sept. 1972).

Shaw, Clifford R., and McKay, Henry D. Social Factors in Juvenile Delinquency. "Report on the Causes of Crime," National Commission on Law Enforcement, No. 13, Vol. II. Government Printing Office, 1931.

Sterling, Joanne W. and Harty, Robert W. "An Alternative Model of Community Services for Ex-Offenders," Federal Probation, Vol. 36 (Sept. 1972).

Taft, Donald R. "Influence of the General Culture on Crime," Federal Probation, Vol. XXX (September 1966).

Thompson, Charles B. "A Psychiatric Study of Recidivists, "American Journal of Psychiatry, (November 1937).

Tucker, Sterling. "The Ghetto, The Ghettoized, and Crime," Federal Probation, Vol. XXXIII (September 1969).

Vehling, Harold F. "Crime Breeds on Smothered Feelings," Federal Probation, Vol. XXX (March 1966).

West, Alexander Van. "Cultural Background and Treatment of the Persistent Offender," Federal Probation. Vol. XXVIII (June 1964).